U.S. MARINE CORPS
WOMEN'S RESERVE
'THEY ARE MARINES'

'These female Marines are part of the Marine Corps Reserve,
itself part of the United States Marine Corps, and therefore
THEY ARE MARINES
and will be referred to as such by all at all times.'
Lieutenant General Thomas Holcomb, Commandant, USMC

U.S. MARINE CORPS

WOMEN'S RESERVE
'THEY ARE MARINES!'
THE USMCWR IN WORLD WAR II

JIM MORAN

FOREWORD BY NANCY WILT,
UNITED STATES MARINE 1970–1982

FRONTLINE BOOKS
An imprint of Pen & Sword Books Ltd
Yorkshire - Philadelphia

First published in Great Britain in 2018 by Frontline Books

An imprint of Pen & Sword Books Ltd
Yorkshire – Philadelphia

Copyright © Jim Moran, 2018

2018 Hardback ISBN 978-1-52671-045-1
2019 Paperback ISBN 978-1-52674-905-5

The right of Jim Moran to be identified as the author of this work has been asserted by him in accordance with the Copyright, Designs and Patents Act 1988.

A CIP catalogue record for this book is available from the British Library
All rights reserved. No part of this book may be reproduced or transmitted in any form or by any means, electronic or mechanical including photocopying, recording or by any information storage and retrieval system, without permission from the Publisher in writing.

Typeset in Sabon and Gill Sans

Printed and bound in India by Replika Press Pvt. Ltd.
Designed and typeset by Ian Hughes, www.mousematdesign.com

For more information on our books, please visit
www.frontline-books.com, email info@frontline-books.com
For a complete list of Pen & Sword titles please contact

PEN & SWORD BOOKS LTD
47 Church Street, Barnsley, South Yorkshire, S70 2AS, England
E-mail: enquiries@pen-and-sword.co.uk
Website: www.pen-and-sword.co.uk
Or
PEN AND SWORD BOOKS
1950 Lawrence Rd, Havertown, PA 19083, USA
E-mail: Uspen-and-sword@casematepublishers.com
Website: www.penandswordbooks.com

CONTENTS

Dedication	7
Acknowledgements	14
Foreword by Nancy Wilt	15
Introduction	17

1. US Marine Corps Women's Reserve — 21
Training of Women Reservists – Officer Training – Recruit Training – Clothing Instructions – Transfer to New River – Troop Trains – 'Hometown' Platoons – Training at Camp Lejeune – Specialist Training – Promotion from the Ranks – Reserve Officer Class

2. Jobs and Job Assignments — 43
Job Classification – Promotion – Jobs in Aviation

3. Administration and Policies — 46
Cooperation with the Women's Services – Policy about Assignment and Housing – Assistants for the Women's Reserve – Policy about Women's Authority – Changing Policy on Marriage

4. Specialist Units and Decorations — 50
The Women's Reserve Band – Quantico's Drill Team – Decorations Awarded to Women Marines

5. Hawaii Duty — 52
Selection of Women for Overseas Duty – Advance Party – Staging Area and Arrival in Hawaii

6. Demobilisation — 59
Strength at End of the War – Last Days of the Wartime Reserve

Chronology – USMCWR — 62

THE UNIFORMS — 65

HEADWEAR — 93

ACCESSORIES — 99

APPENDIX 1. Quartermaster Photographs   109

APPENDIX 2. Jobs in Which Women Marines Were Assigned During WWII   148

APPENDIX 3. Buttons   151

APPENDIX 4. Memo to Lillian Sandy   156

APPENDIX 5. Uniforms and Accessories, MCWR – Issues and Quantities Contracted   160

APPENDIX 6. Uniforms and Accessories, MCWR – Required Items   162

APPENDIX 7. Uniforms and Accessories, MCWR – List of Specifications   164

APPENDIX 8. Uniform Regulations 1943   167

APPENDIX 9. Uniform Regulations 1945   185

'THEY ARE MARINES'

THE USMC WOMEN'S RESERVE IN WORLD WAR II

In memory of

LILLIAN SANDY MITTELSDORF

And all the women of America who 'freed a Marine to fight'

SEMPER FIDELIS

Lillian Marie Sandy (Mittelsdorf)

Lillian enlisted into the Marine Corps Women's Reserve in Kansas City, Missouri, on 19 November 1943 at the age of 20. She attended induction and recruit training (boot camp) at Camp Lejeune, New River, North Carolina, after which she was assigned to Motor Transport School (MTS) for truck driving and automotive mechanic's training. On completion of this training, Lillian was assigned as an assistant driving instructor.

It was whilst stationed at Lejeune that Lillian met Joe Mittelsdorf, a welding instructor at the MTS. They became good friends and would eventually marry in August of 1947. When permission was granted for Marine WRs to serve outside continental USA, Lillian volunteered for overseas duty and was assigned as Secretary in the Motor Transport Division and driver to the MTD Colonel in charge, Pearl Harbor, HI.

Lillian was stationed at Pearl Harbor for the remainder of the war, was transferred to Marine Air Base, El Toro, CA in 1945 and was honourably discharged on 28 December 1945.

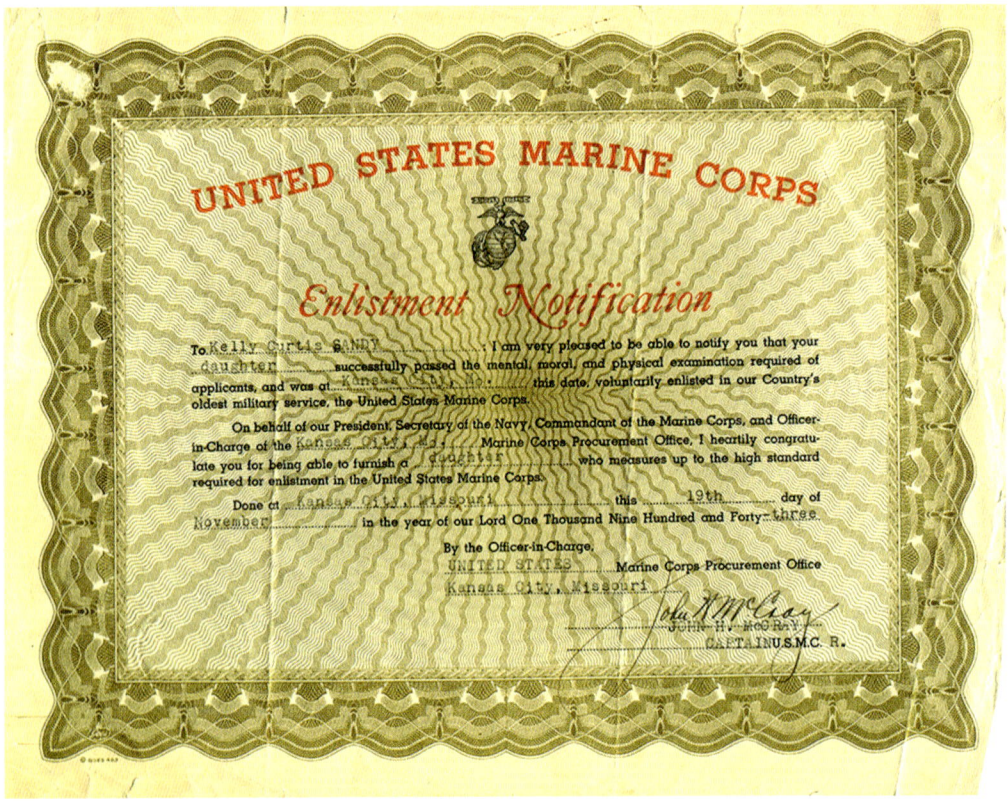

Enlistment notification sent to Lillian's parents

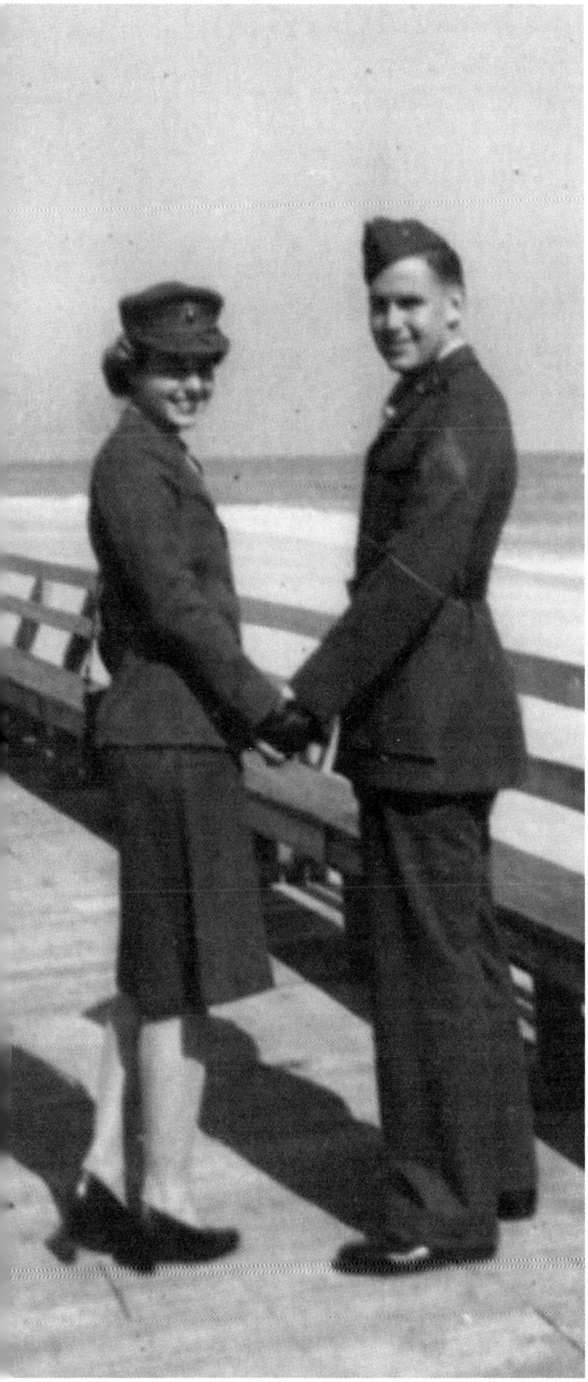

Above: Joe and Lillian on a rare day off at Lejeune; both are in winter service dress

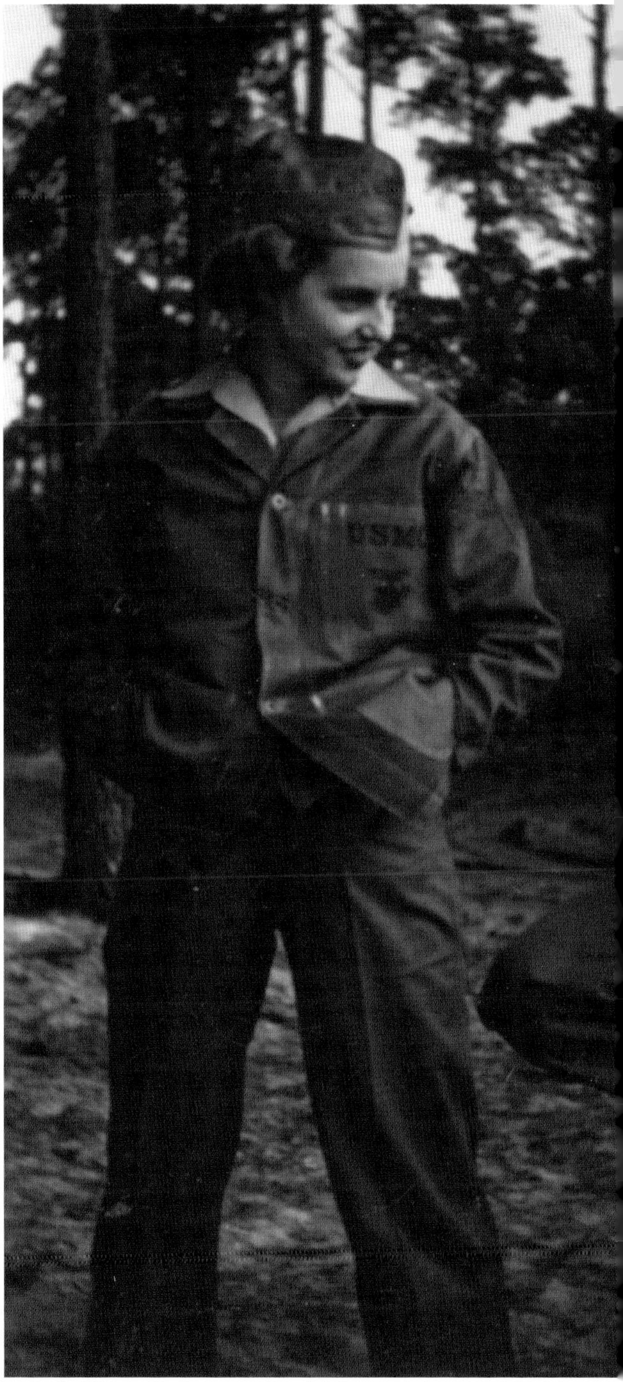

Above: Uniform of the day at MTS was always work dungarees! WR dungarees were too lightweight for mechanic work so Lillian was issued men's dungarees, as were all the WRs in MTS

Above: On a rare occasion, Lillian gets to wear her winter service uniform at Lejeune

Above: Lillian with her best friend at MTS Camp Lejeune – both wear women's shirts with men's dungaree trousers and garrison caps

Above: 'Welcome to Hawaii' – Lillian, like all the other WRs, received a lei greeting as she disembarked from the transport ship

Above: Lillian at last gets to wear her summer dress whites in Hawaii

Above right: On Hawaii, summer dress whites was the uniform of the day

Right: Photo of Lillian carried by Joe through the Pacific (the bracelet Lillian is wearing was made for her by Joe)

LILLIAN MARIE SANDY (MITTELDORF)

ACKNOWLEDGEMENTS

Once again, as in my previous books, many people have given of their valuable time in the production of this book. In particular, I would like to thank the following:

First and foremost, much of the detailed information on the Women's Reserve in World War II was provided from the 1968 Historical Branch, G-3 Division, Headquarters, US Marine Corps, by Lieutenant Colonel Pat Meid, USMCR. Also from Headquarters, US Marine Corps is the Quartermaster General's *History of the Marine Corps Women's Reserve, MCWR Uniforms and Accessories, September 1945*. These detailed reports were supplied by Nancy Wilt of the Women Marines Association. Nancy is also keeper of the Women of the Corps Collection and has provided a great deal of her valuable time in accommodating and feeding me, my wife and daughter, and allowing me to photograph many rare WR items.

Thanks also go to the Marine Corps Histories Division, Quantico, Virginia, and to Owen Connor, Uniforms and Heraldry Curator, National Museum of the Marine Corps. To the Alfred M. Gray Marine Corps Research Center (GRC), Quantico, VA, and, in particular, Mike Miller, for providing many of the period photographs.

Special thanks go to Major 'Rick' Spooner, USMC (Ret.) for his long-lasting support for my efforts; to Captain Ned Wilt, USMC (Ret.) – long-suffering husband of Nancy – for keeping us fed, watered and entertained throughout our stay with them; to Joe and Carol Mittelsdorf for sharing their memories of their wife and mother Lillian Sandy; and to Lillian herself for sharing her times as a woman Marine in WWII (guard those streets well Marine).

Finally, I would like to thank Mike Allen, USMC (Ret.), founder Commandant US Marine Corps League, Detachment 1088 (UK) for his help and encouragement in researching this book.

'I wish you all fair winds and following seas.'

Production was by Gavin Douse, modelling and photography by Tara Moran, David Massey and Margaret Moran.

My thanks to all.

Semper Fi

Jim Moran

FOREWORD

A generation of Americans has grown to maturity largely unaware of the political, social and military implications of World War II – a war that, more than any other, brought all of us Americans together with a common purpose.

American women had served with distinction in the US Marine Corps, US Navy and the US Coast Guard during World War I, and their superior service proved that women could be major assets in times of war and conflict. Women Marines in WWI held the name of United States Marine Corps Reserve Female (USMCRFs).

At the end of the war the US military discharged their women – perhaps believing that the war 'to end all wars' would allow them to return to hearth and home. However, the wartime service of American women in the nation's military, as well as in manufacturing, business, education and so on helped to ensure the passage of the 19th Amendment, which gave women the right to vote in 1920.

In World War II, the majority of women's services in the United States were formed, starting in mid-1942, as auxiliaries to the male services. The Marine Corps opened recruiting for women on 13 February 1943 but, unlike their sister services, they did not create an auxiliary, nor did they have a modified or catchy name, like the WAVES of the United States Navy, the WACs of the United States Army or the SPARS of the United States Coast Guard. Women who joined the Corps were United States Marines, sharing 168 years of tradition and esprit de corps with their male counterparts.

An unknown Marine in World War II was quoted as describing the women of the United States Marine Corps Women's Reserve (USMCWR) as 'the smallest sorority in the biggest fraternity in the world'. That small sorority of 1940s women who volunteered, earned the title Marine and then worked in over 225 occupational fields, filling positions that allowed the critically needed manpower, planes and equipment to reach the battlefields of the Pacific. The women had their illustrious Eagle, Globe and Anchor and wore the distinctive Forest Green of the US Marines – they were Marines.

The high standards and respect of the American public toward the United States Marine Corps as being the 'best of the best' soon extended to include the women who now held the title of United States Marine, securing many USMCWR members and the women who followed a permanent place in the United States Marine Corps.

2018 marks 100 years since the United States Marine Corps accepted women into their ranks, and women Marines have served with pride and distinction in each decade since 1918. It is therefore significant that this book is being published in the centennial year of women in the United States Marine Corps.

James, thank you for honoring the Women Marines of the WWII era and all women who have served or are currently serving as United States Marines.

Semper Fidelis

Nancy Wilt
United States Marine 1970–1982
Curator of the Women of the Corps Collection
Women Marine Historian
2018

INTRODUCTION

Marine folklore tells that, when at a dinner party in October 1942, Major General Commandant Thomas Holcomb announced to the guests present that he had authorised the acceptance of women into the Marine Corps Reserve, the portrait of 5th Commandant of the Marine Corps, Archibald Henderson, fell from the wall and crashed to the floor in disbelief!

Women in the Marine Corps was not totally unheard of; Lucy Brewer served as Marine Gunner George Baker aboard the USS *Constitution* during the war of 1812, being honourably discharged in 1815 with her female identity undiscovered. During World War I some 300 women served as USMC(F) (or Marinettes as they were referred to by the media of the time), mainly at Marine Corps Headquarters in Washington, DC. The first known woman to enlist was Opha May Johnson, who joined on 13 August 1918.

From the outset, following the public announcement of the new Women's Reserve in February of 1943, public media showed great interest in these female Marines, the Marine Corps being the last of the armed services to enlist women into their ranks. The media wanted all details of the 'Lady Leathernecks', as they christened them: What were they like? What jobs would they undertake

WWI Marinettes, Washington, DC

from male Marines? What would they wear? What would they be called? The Army had their WACs, the Navy their WAVES and the Coast Guard their SPARS, so 'what will we call these female Marines?' they asked. The reply from the Marine Corps was not necessarily to their liking when, in an article in *Life* magazine, Major General Holcomb commented,

> They are Marines. They don't have a nickname and they don't need one. They get their basic training in a Marine atmosphere at a Marine Post. They inherit the traditions of Marines. They are Marines!

The media was not put off by this, suggesting titles such as 'Lady Leathernecks', 'MARS', 'Femarines', 'WAMs', 'Dainty Devil Dogs', even 'Sub Marines'. They settled on the nickname of 'BAMs' – Beautiful American Marines. Unfortunately, BAMs was quickly interpreted by the female Marines' male counterparts into 'Broad Ass Marines', allegedly due to the fact that on a standard 2.5-ton cargo truck you could sit eight male Marines but only seven female Marines. This caused great friction between the male and female Marines, and was only resolved by the intervention of Major General Commandant Holcomb who issued a directive that 'These female Marines are part of the Marine Corps Reserve, itself part of the United States Marine Corps, and therefore they are Marines and will be referred to as such by all at all times.' (Although the female Marines were often referred to as Women Reservists or WRs.)

Although unpopular at first, by 1945 Women Marines had 'released a man to fight' in sufficient numbers to allow the Marine Corps to field the 6th Marine Division, made up primarily of veteran Marines, in time for the invasion of Okinawa on 1 April 1945.

Marinettes on recruitment drive in 1918

Lucy Brewer

INTRODUCTION

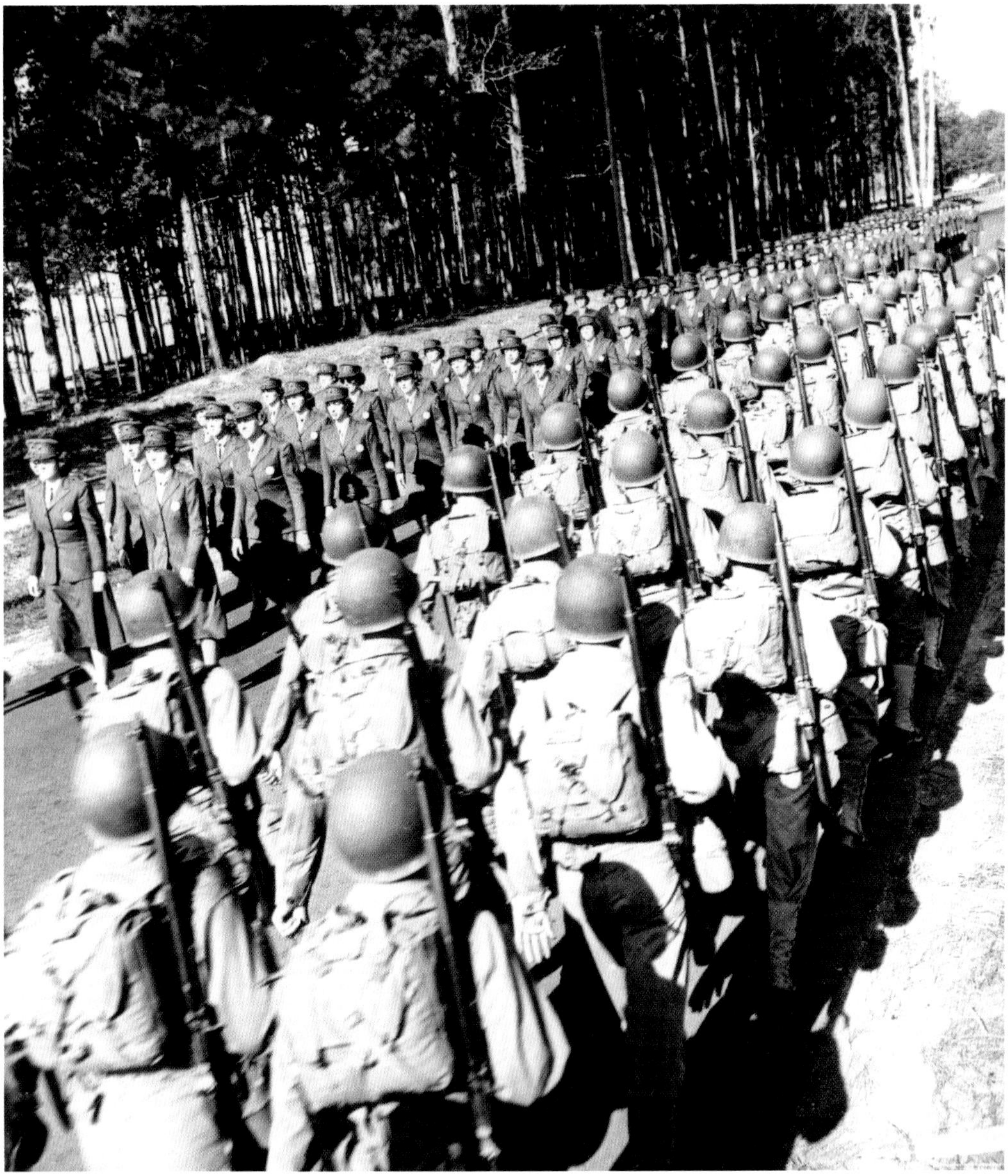

'Free a Marine to fight'

CHAPTER 1

US MARINE CORPS WOMEN'S RESERVE

On 7 November 1942, just three days before the 167th birthday of the Marine Corps, the Marine Corps Commandant, Lieutenant General Thomas Holcomb, gave his official approval to the formation of the Marine Corps Women's Reserve. During the next three years, more than 20,000 women would serve in the WR, releasing urgently needed male Marines for combat duty. Marine Corps Headquarters quickly went about setting up the policies and procedures needed to initiate this move, however, the official announcement was not made to the American public until three months later – 13 February 1943. The Marine Corps had tried to avoid making the announcement before the plans were fully developed, as they felt that this would not be in the best interest of the newly formed Women's Reserve.

The Marine Corps was the last of the four services to set up a women's reserve in World War II. It was widely believed that the Commandant of the Marine Corps had been against the formation of a Women's Reserve, even though the Women's Army Auxiliary Corps (WAAC) and the Navy's Women Accepted for Volunteer Emergency Service (WAVES) were being developed. Less than a year after the Women Marines had been formed, he commented, 'Like most other Marines, when the matter first came up I didn't believe women could serve any useful purpose in the Marine Corps . . . Since then I've changed my mind.'

General Holcomb realised, however, that when the matter of a Women's Reserve was brought for discussion as a serious possibility in World War II, the admission of Women Marines would be on a greater scale than had been previously envisaged, and would raise numerous new questions and problems, all of which would require an answer or solution.

The decision to admit women to the Marine Corps came about as the result of studies carried out by the M-1 section of the Plans and Policies Division at Marine Corps Headquarters. Although the matter had been discussed months earlier, it had been dropped due to the Commandant's feelings on the subject. When it was realised that it would release urgently needed combat personnel in large numbers, the debate was re-opened and re-studied.

On 5 October 1942, the Plans and Policies Division recommended that the Women's Reserve be established and suggested to the Commandant that it be a separate section within the Division of Reserve. The Commandant agreed and, on 12 October, wrote to the Secretary of the Navy,

> In furtherance of the war effort, it was believed that as many women as possible should be used in non-combatant billets, thus releasing a greater number of the limited manpower available for essential combat duty.

He quoted Public Law 689, 77th Congress, approved on 30 July 1942, which amended the Naval Reserve Act of 1938 by the addition of a section entitled 'Women's Reserve' and stating that it should be part of the Naval Reserve.

On 26 October, the first endorsement of the Commandant's letter by the Judge Advocate General's office approved this, stating,

> The creation of a Women's Reserve, which shall be a branch of the United States Marine Corps Reserve, appears to be fully authorised by the law. The specific proposals of the Commandant of the Marine Corps as contained in the basic communication have been examined in this office and it is considered that they legally be approved.

The second endorsement came on 30 October from the Commander in Chief, United States Fleet and Chief of Naval Operations, and was equally approving. Final authorisation for the creation of the Women's Reserve from Secretary of the Navy, Frank Knox, was received on 31 October, followed by that of President Franklin D. Roosevelt on 7 November. Authorisation was for an initial force of 500 officers and 6,000 enlisted by 30 June 1943, increasing to a total of 1,000 officers and 18,000 enlisted by 30 June 1944.

The distribution of rank and grade was the same as for the men of the Marine Corps and based on the number of women to be enlisted: the allocation of officers was 1 Major and 35 Captains, with 35% of the total number of commissioned officers to be in the rank of First Lieutenant and the remainder to be Second Lieutenants. Determination of the highest rank held by a member of the Marine Corps Women's Reserve was based on Public Law 689, which provided for one officer with the rank of Lieutenant Commander for the Women's Reserve of the United States Naval Reserve. The counterpart in the Marine Corps would hold the rank of Major. Subsequent amendments to the law would increase the rank of the senior woman in each naval service to Captain (Navy and Coast Guard) and Colonel (Marine Corps).

The first distinct step towards establishing the Women's Reserve was made on 5 November 1942, when the Commandant wrote to commanding officers in all Marine posts and procurement districts, announcing that the Marine Corps was 'initiating steps to organise a Women's Reserve'. He directed all officers to review activities within their jurisdiction and identify the number of Women Reservists (WRs) who could replace officers and men in areas such as clerical, communications, transportation, mess and commissary, mechanical and so on. He explained that, 'within the next year the manpower shortage will be such that it will be incumbent on all concerned with the national welfare to replace men by women in all possible positions'. From the information returned from posts and stations, projections were made of the number of women who would need specialist training in fields such as Paymaster, Quartermaster and Communications, in addition to estimates of WRs who could effectively use the skills they would be bringing to the Marine Corps from civilian life. Quotas were established for recruitment of enlisted women and officers, and tentative start dates were identified for training classes.

Although the Marine Corps was only authorised for a strength of 6,500 women by 30 June 1943, the findings from this preliminary survey suggested that more than 4,000 would be needed immediately. The numbers of WRs requested by Marine Corps stations were:

Quantico, Virginia	692
Cherry Point, North Carolina	688
Camp Lejeune, New River, North Carolina	726
San Diego, California	650
Camp Elliott, California	981
Camp Pendleton, California	416
Parris Island, South Carolina	278
Total	4,431

A considerable amount of pre-planning was required to ensure successful recruitment, training, administration and equipping of the new Women's Reserve. One of the most important tasks, however, was the selection and appointment of a Director. The Commandant was in no doubt that the success of the Women's Reserve would depend on the calibre and capability of the woman chosen for this post, and in November he wrote to Dean Virginia C. Gildersleeve of Barnard College, Columbia University, to enlist her help. The Commandant wrote, in part:

> It is my understanding that in the selection of the woman to head up the WAVES, the Navy availed itself of the advice of the Advisory Educational Council, of which you are the Chairman. If it is not too much of an imposition, the Marine Corps would be glad if your Council could undertake a similar service for it.

General Holcomb was quick to point out that the Marine Corps did not intend to dictate the method by which candidates were chosen, whether this was decided by sub-committee or by any other means:

> We are only interested in procuring the services of some woman who is qualified for a commission as Major in the Marine Corps and to assume the parallel position to Miss McAfee (Lieutenant Commander Mildred McAfee, Director of the WAVES).

Soon afterwards, Dean Gildersleeve and her committee presented a recommendation of 12 outstanding women and the Marine Corps began making discreet enquiries on their capabilities. The candidates were interviewed in person by the Director of Reserve, Colonel Littleton W. T. Waller, Jr, under whose office the Women's Reserve would be held for administrative purposes. Colonel Waller and his right-hand man, Major C. Brewster Rhoads, travelled across the country to interview prospective candidates individually, their recommendations leading eventually to the selection of Mrs Ruth Cheney Streeter, age 47, of Morristown, New Jersey.

Mrs Streeter was President of her class at Bryn Mawr College, the mother of four grown up children including two sons in the Navy and one in the Army, and

Colonel Littleton Waller

Major Ruth Streeter

was active in health and welfare work in New Jersey for over 20 years. She was a strong-willed woman who had, within the previous year, taken out both private and commercial pilot's licences and was considered to have the combination of personal and organisational abilities required of a Woman Marine Director. Mrs Streeter was commissioned a Major, USMCWR, on 29 January 1943, sworn in by Secretary of the Navy, Knox.

In regard to procurement and training, the existing facilities of the WAVES would be used as much as possible, according to a joint letter to the Secretary of the Navy from the Chief of Naval Personnel and the Commandants of the Marine Corps and the Coast Guard. As the Women's Reserves of both the Marine Corps and the Coast Guard were part of the Naval establishment, the official recommendation was that members of these units be procured through the Office of Naval Officer Procurement and trained 'insofar as it is practical' in schools already set up for members of the WAVES.

In February 1943 six other women, in addition to Major Streeter and Captain Lentz, had been directly commissioned from civilian life before the official public announcement of the Women's Reserve. Lentz was commissioned to design the various uniforms for the WRs and commissioned Captain on 15 January 1943. All had been selected because their abilities and experience equipped them for key Marine Corps billets, such as recruitment and training, which had to be filled right away. They commenced duty at Marine Corps Headquarters immediately, commissioned without any formal induction and in civilian clothing. These Marines were:

Women's Reserve representative for Public Relations
– First Lieutenant E. Louise Stewart
Women's Reserve representative for Training
– Captain Charlotte D. Gower
Women's Reserve representative for Classification and Detail
– Captain Cornelia D. T. Williams
Women's Reserve representative for West Coast Activities
– Captain Lillian O'Malley Daly
Women's Reserve representative for Recruit Depot
– Captain Katherine A. Towle
Women's Reserve Assistant to the Director
– Captain Helen C. O'Neill.

Three major factors favoured the Marine Corps Women's Reserve, despite the fact that they were the last of the women's wartime services to be established. These were:

First – the Marines shared their proud name, spanning 168 years of tradition and *esprit de corps*. They therefore became Women Marines and did not have an abbreviation of their designation or semi-official nickname, in spite of the public media's attempts!

Second – the Women's Reserve was accepted as a full-fledged integrated part of the Marine Corps and not an auxiliary service.

Third – the men's distinctive forest green uniform was followed closely, with modifications to 'feminise' for the Women Marines. In the same way as the name Marines, this gave to the Women Marines the feeling of acceptance on an equal basis in the Marine Corps and encouraged hard work and dedication to ensure they deserved the name 'good Marines'.

In a recommendation to the Commandant one month before the announcement of the Women's Reserve was made to the public, Colonel Waller, Director of Reserve, declared:

> Women Reservists of the US Marine Corps will not be specially designated as in the case of WAVES or SPARS, but will be called Marines. It is proposed that they will be uniformed in the forest green of the Marine Corps with suitable differences being made in the material and in the cut of the uniform to conform to the convenience and smart appearance of women, but sufficiently like the Marine Corps uniform to permit no possibility of doubt as to the branch of the service to which the Women Reservists are attached.

The first official announcement of the Women's Reserve to the general public was made on 13 February 1943 and Navy procurement offices throughout the country that had been made responsible for enlistment were swamped with women who wanted to be Marines. In Washington, DC, over 100 applications were filed during the first two days after enlistment opened, causing one recruiting officer to complain that the overload of applicants was causing his office staff to 'get behind in their work'.

Applications were received from a wide range of women, from Mrs Otho L. Rogers of Washington, DC, and Mrs Henry T. Elrod of Coronado, California, both widows of Marine Majors recently killed in combat, to schoolgirls, office workers, grandmothers and college students. Enthusiasm was so high that some women tried to enlist on the Saturday when the initial announcement was made, even though enlistments did not officially open until the following Monday. Indeed, records show that some of them succeeded. With the exception of the few officers direct-commissioned before the public announcement, the distinction of being the first World War II Woman Marine went to Lucille E. McClarren of Nemacolin, Pennsylvania, who enlisted in Washington, DC, on 13 February.

Eligibility requirements both for enlisted and officers were that they hold United States citizenship, not be married to a Marine, and must be either single or, if married, have no children under 18. They must be at least 60 inches in height and not less than 95 pounds in weight, and have good teeth and vision. For enlisted (also called general service) the age requirement was 20 to 35 inclusive and candidates must have had at least two years of high school. In regard to officer candidates, the entry requirements were initially the same as WAVES and SPARS, i.e. between 20 and 49 years of age and either a college graduate or having a combination of two years' college and two years' work experience.

From the start, the Marine Corps struggled to cope with the number of volunteers and readily accepted the offer from the Navy Department to second some WAVES officers currently in training to assist with the recruitment process. Several WAVES volunteered and the Marine Corps chose 19, one for each of their procurement offices across the country. These WAVES were sworn in as Marines and transferred immediately to the job of recruiting Women Marines. However, they still wore their WAVES uniforms since the Marine Corps uniforms were not yet available.

Through the busy early months, the traditional improvisation characteristic to the Marine Corps was needed and in some of the larger cities Marine officers requested permission from Headquarters to enlist civilian women to help with the growing mountain of paperwork. Many of the requests were

PAY AND RANK OF THE WOMEN'S RESERVE

OFFICERS: Rank	Monthly Base Pay	Without Dependents	Rent Sub-allow.
Colonel	$333.33	*$105.00	$21.00
Lieut. Colonel	291.67	105.00	21.00
Major	250.00	90.00	21.00
Captain	200.00	75.00	21.00
1st Lieutenant	166.67	60.00	21.00
2nd Lieutenant	150.00	45.00	21.00

* Note: Officers who are assigned to quarters furnished by the Government or officers on duty at a post or station with troops, are not entitled to rental allowance.

Rank	ENLISTED PERSONNEL	Monthly Base Pay (Plus Allowance)
Sergeant Major, First Sergeant, Master Gunnery Sergeant, Master Technical Sergeant, Quartermaster Sergeant, Paymaster Sergeant, Master Steward, Master Cook	First Pay Grade	$138.00
Gunnery Sergeant, Technical Sergeant, Drum Major, Supply Sergeant, Steward 1st Class, Cook 1st Class	Second Pay Grade	114.00
Platoon Sergeant, Staff Sergeant, Steward 2nd Class, Cook 2nd Class	Third Pay Grade	96.00
Sergeant, Mess Sergeant, Chief Cook, Field Music Sergeant, Steward 3rd Class, Cook 3rd Class	Fourth Pay Grade	78.00
Corporal, Field Cook, Field Music Corporal, Steward's Asst. 1st Class	Fifth Pay Grade	66.00
Private 1st Class, Assistant Cook, Field Music 1st Class, Steward's Asst. 2nd Class	Sixth Pay Grade	54.00
Private, Field Music, Steward's Asst. 3rd Class	Seventh Pay Grade	50.00

In addition to the Base Pay, the Marine Corps provides free to all enlisted Marines, men and women, food and living accommodations, or, where food and living accommodations are not furnished by the Marine Corps, a quarters allowance of $1.25 per day and a subsistence allowance of $1.80 per day with which to provide these accommodations.

Women Marines and their dependents are eligible for allowances similar in most respects to those provided enlisted men.

Low cost Post Exchange Stores reduce considerably the cost of personal spending, and you have free mail privileges, discounts from railroads, theatres and many restaurants, hotels and clubs.

WR pay and rank

granted and the women commenced duty immediately, receiving their formal indoctrination as Women Marines at a later date.

For the purpose of procurement, the country was divided into four major districts, and candidates for both officer and recruit (boot) training were enlisted by naval procurement offices in each of these districts. Newly enlisted women were on 'inactive duty' pending the processing of their applications by Marine Corps Headquarters. They were then notified to which training class they had been assigned. Designations were either Class VI(a) officer or Class VI(b) enlisted. Male categories of the Reserve were:

Class I – Fleet Marine Corps Reserve
Class II – Organised Marine Corps Reserve
Class III – Volunteer Marine Corps Reserve
Class IV – Limited Service Marine Corps Reserve
Class V – Specialist Volunteer Marine Corps Reserve

Applicants had to provide a physical statement from their own physician, complete and return the application to the recruiting station, take an aptitude test and a complete physical, and have a personal interview with the officer in charge. A statement of the woman's capabilities and value to the service would then be prepared by him, and the final decision on whether to accept a candidate was made by Headquarters Marine Corps. If the candidate was considered to be well qualified, a waiver for lack of a particular physical or educational item could be applied.

The Marine Corps Reserve Reviewing Board were very selective, rejecting around 25% of applications from procurement offices for officer candidate class. Commenting on the first month of the new women's service, Colonel Waller stated:

> The women of the country have responded in just the manner we expected ... Thousands of women have volunteered to serve in the Women's Reserve and from them we have already selected more than 1,000 for the enlisted ranks and over 100 as officers.

WRs on recruit drive 1943

The targeted maximum number to be enrolled up to 1 July was 6,000 enlisted and 500 officers.

Major Streeter made a nationwide trip during this first month of the Women's Reserve, visiting 16 major cities from coast to coast, in addition to the Marine Corps posts where her women would be serving. She addressed a number of public gatherings, including women's clubs and college assemblies and noted a 'spontaneous enthusiasm among women for the new women's service organisation'. On her return to Washington on 26 March from one of her many trips into the field, she commented: 'The privilege of swearing in many enlistees gave me an opportunity to observe the young women joining our ranks. I found them to be most sincere, intelligent and attractive representatives of American young womanhood.'

There was a total of 2,495 enlistments to the Women's Reserve in the first eight weeks, of which 28 were on active duty, 211 enrolled in officer candidates class and the remainder in recruit training or awaiting orders for active duty. Thus, in the first two months almost one-seventh of the total enlisted and over one quarter of the future officers had been enrolled. In one area, the procurement officer in charge commented:

> While it is not properly a concern of this office, it is felt that the Division of Reserve might well consider decreasing the overall publicity given to the Women's program, since the number of applications far exceeds the authorised quotas. It is considered to be bad public relations by this office when unavoidable circumstances necessitate turning away many desirable

First arrivals at Mount Holyoke College

New arrivals at Hunters College

and well-qualified applicants who have been encouraged to believe that their enlistment could be effected.

Marine recruiters had always carried out enlistment procedures for the male Marines, but by July 1943 responsibility for the women was passed on to them from the naval procurement offices. Physical examinations, however, remained the responsibility of the Navy. By 1 November 1943, more than 11,000 officers and enlisted personnel had been sworn in – less than 1,000 off the 12,000 quota set for 1 January 1944. Of these, around 8,500 had been classified and were already on duty. In February 1944, only one year after its formation, the Women's Reserve totalled nearly 15,000. In that year the number of officers had increased from 4 to 800 and the number of enlisted women stood at 14,000. The Director stated in 1944:

> It is anticipated that by 31 May the Marine Corps Women's Reserve will have reached its total authorised strength. Although our quota is much smaller than those of the WACs (Women's Army Corps) or WAVES, the fact still remains that, though we were the last of the women's military services to be organised, we are the first to succeed in enlisting all the women we can presently use. Furthermore, we reached our goal in two and a half months less time than we expected. The original plan called for recruiting to start on 1 January 1943 and proceed at the rate of 1,000 per month until 30 June 1944. Actually, we did not start until 15 February 1943 and reached our quota on 31 May 1944, thus accomplishing our mission in fifteen and a half months instead of eighteen.

Training of Women Reservists

In addition to assistance with recruitment, the Navy offered the use of its training facilities for officers and enlisted personnel in the early days of the Women's

Hunters College

'Pass in Review' – WRs at Hunters College

Reserve. This saved a substantial amount of time for the Marine Corps, who would have suffered a delay of several months had it been necessary to train their own staff for women's schools. This would have caused an onward delay in releasing men for combat. Officers and enlisted classes began in March 1943 at Mount Holyoke College (officers) and Hunter College (enlisted).

Officer Training
On 13 March 1943, one month after the public announcement of the Women's Reserve, 71 officer candidates entered US Naval Midshipmen's School (WR) in Northampton, Massachusetts, to commence training with the WAVES. The Midshipmen's School consisted of the facilities of Smith College, Northampton, and Mount Holyoke, South Hadley, where Marine candidates received their initial training. The class included a variety of civilian roles such as educators, scientists, secretaries and women from businesses and professions.

Marine officer candidates followed the same course as the WAVES for the first

Class Review, 1st Platoon Hunters College

Drill field – note male drill instructors

US MARINES CORPS WOMEN'S RESERVE

half of the training, which lasted approximately four weeks. Subjects included Naval Organisation and Administration, Naval Personnel, Naval History and Strategy, Naval Law and Justice, Ships and Aircraft. The second part was separate from the WAVES and consisted of Marine Corps subjects such as Marine Corps Administration and Courtesies, Map Reading, Interior Guard, Safeguarding Military Information and Physical Training. The courses were delivered by Marine Corps instructors. Like all Marine recruits, the women were schooled by male Marine Drill Instructors who were transferred specifically from Parris Island Recruit Depot.

On 6 April the members of the first class received their silver OC pins, marking the promotion to officer cadet. This specially created category, authorised by the Secretary of the Navy, corresponded to the status and pay rating of their WAVES contemporaries and was designed to give some parity since the Navy candidates went through training as midshipmen. Successful candidates received commissions on 4 May, just over seven weeks after entering; the second candidates class began training on 10 April; and the third in early May. A total of 214 Women Marines completed officer training at Mount Holyoke, with a new class entering each month.

In administrative terms, the Marine training unit had the same status as a Marine detachment aboard ship, the women having their own commanding officer who had responsibility for discipline and for coordinating drill instruction and academic subjects with the school. Marine candidates were organised into separate companies under the immediate command of an officer of the regular Marine Corps, Major E. Hunter Hurst. The WR detachment was, however, part of the WAVES school under the final authority of the commanding officer of the Midshipmen's School.

All officer candidates enlisted as privates, and, following their initial four-week training, those women not qualified for appointment as cadets could either be transferred to Hunter College to complete basic training, or be ordered to their

Typical WR barracks

Newly arrived WRs at Camp Lejeune

home with inactive status, to await discharge from the Marine Corps. Cadets who were not recommended for commissioned rank on completion of training resigned officially to the Commandant and were discharged. They were able to re-enlist as private provided they met the age requirement.

Recruit training

Two weeks after the first officer class, the first class of 722 enlisted women started their training at Hunter College in the Bronx, New York, officially the US Naval Training School. The members of this class arrived over a three-day period from 24 to 26 March in three equal daily groups. The 'boots' were billeted in apartment houses nearby and began instruction with the WAVES on 26 March. The administrative arrangements were similar to Mount Holyoke but much larger. Marine recruits were separated into companies, each one headed by a male Marine officer and combined into a battalion under Major William W. Buchanan. This first class was divided into 21 platoons, with approximately 35 women in each.

Dispensary – Camp Lejeune

Admin building – Camp Lejeune

US MARINES CORPS WOMEN'S RESERVE

Captain Katharine A. Towle was on Major Buchanan's staff from the outset and other women were added after the first candidates' class had been commissioned. The Major's staff consisted of 33 instructors – 10 officers and 23 enlisted – who gave instruction on both the Marine Corps and general subjects, working to a similar curriculum to the one at Holyoke. Close-order drill for all women in the training school, both Marines and WAVES, was supervised by a group of 15–20 male drill instructors.

In the first group of enlisted women there were several stenographers, secretaries, telephone operators, laboratory technicians, woodcraft workers, two motor mechanics, one acetylene welder, a commercial artist, a parachute maker and others with occupational and civilian skills. The first class graduated on 25 April 1943, with following classes entering every two weeks, each one having 525 recruits. Indoctrination was around four weeks, but varied between classes due to linking with the WAVES' schedules. Between 26 March and 10 July, six recruit classes were entered with 3,280 Women Marines graduating. Training was intense and fast-paced, however the fallout rate was only 2 per cent.

Officer cadet

Officer USMCWR – note spruce green shoulder boards

Clothing Instructions
Members of the first candidates' class and recruit class undertook half their training in civilian clothes, since uniforms were only issued in late April. Prospective WRs had been issued with detailed instructions before leaving home on the clothing they should bring with them (see Appendix 4). This list included two pairs of comfortable, dark brown, laced Oxfords as, according to the instructions, 'Experience has proven that drilling tends to enlarge the feet'. Trainees were further instructed to ensure they had their orders, not arrive before the exact time and date stamped on their official papers and not forget to bring their ration cards.

Transfer to New River – Camp Lejeune
The Marine Corps had its own schools by summer 1943 and although initially under orders to use the existing facilities of the Navy as far as practical for procurement and training, the facilities at both Hunter and Mount Holyoke were under pressure from class sizes.

In July 1943, both officer candidates' class and recruit depot were transferred to Camp Lejeune, New River, North Carolina, joining the specialists' schools, which had been in operation there since May to form the Marine Corps Women's Reserve Schools. Almost 19,000 women underwent training here during the rest of the war.

The third class of officer candidates was commissioned at Mount Holyoke on 29 June, the combined battalion of WAVES and Marines passing in review before Major Streeter; Lieutenant Commander McAfee, Director of the WAVES; and Brigadier General Keller E. Rockey, USMC, Director of the Division of Plans and Policies at Headquarters. Major Streeter commented,

> The candidates presented an excellent battalion review conducted entirely by themselves without any men officers on the field. They made a very good impression in all ways and left Mount Holyoke with good feeling between themselves and the Navy and the college.

The success of the Mount Holyoke experience was considered to be partly due to the fact that its president was a former Marine, evidenced by the Marine Corps letter of appreciation to Dr Roswell G. Hamm, stating, 'Your continual willingness to assist in the formation of policies and to contribute to the comfort of the Marine Corps personnel at Mount Holyoke were largely responsible for the high morale and fine *esprit de corps* of our officer candidates. Your experience as a former Marine made you keenly aware of the vital importance of the work to be done by the Women's Reserve.'

Also on 29 June, members of the fourth class were promoted to the rank of cadet. Two days later, around 70 members of the training class and the staff left in a troop movement to Camp Lejeune and arrived two days after that. Training resumed on 5 July, the class graduating on 7 August. The fifth class, and all following classes, reported directly to Camp Lejeune.

At Hunter College the class of enlisted women completed training early in July; the tenth class reported direct to Camp Lejeune on 12 July and graduated on 15 August. After this, classes of approximately 550 women entered every two weeks

WRs get a ride in a Higgins boat

and graduated around five to six weeks later, as per the previous schedules. At any one time, three classes were in training simultaneously. This new location for training was welcomed by both students and administrative staff and enabled a more thorough Marine Corps indoctrination than had been possible previously. Enlisted women were also given detailed instruction in administrative procedures applicable to their daily work.

One of the highlights of the move to New River, to which no other women's military service had access, was the field demonstrations, where women witnessed the use of mortars, bazookas, flamethrowers, amphibious tractors, landing craft, hand-to-hand combat, camouflage and war dogs. Selected teams of male Marines gave presentations during half-day sessions. The Director of the Women's Reserve commented: 'By showing the women what the men whom they had released for combat faced, their pride in the Corps was increased, and they saw clearly their own part in it.' The introduction of these sessions had been initiated by a letter from Major Hurst, Commanding Officer of the Marine Training Detachment at the Midshipmen's School in South Hadley, received by Brigadier General Waller soon after training began. Extracts from Major Hurst's letter state:

> In drawing these up [training schedules ordered by Marine Corps Headquarters] I found myself wishing more and more that we could include some weapons instructions, at least pistol, for our women . . . I have found that the women come into the Marine Corps expecting to learn to shoot and I, of course, would like to see them become the first women's reserve

Ready to ship out – Camp Lejeune

in the country to take up the specialty of their men, if Headquarters considers the idea at all feasible. I wouldn't have had the nerve to suggest it if Mrs Franklin D. Roosevelt hadn't asked me on her visit last week how soon they were going to learn to shoot. She expressed surprise at learning that the women of the US were not learning as much about weapons as the women of other countries . . .

In a memorandum drafted on 12 June 1943 by Major Streeter, the proposed curricula for the Marine Corps Women's Reserve Schools, due to open in July at New River, were discussed. Major Streeter noted that classes included lectures on combat equipment, landing operations, tactics, parachute troops and amphibious tractors, and suggested,

If it is possible to arrange transportation and schedules that would not interrupt the training of the men in these lines of work, I believe it would be a definite inspiration to the Marine Corps Women's Reserve to see them actually in training.

This suggestion was approved and the women's training amended, a change considered by all concerned to be an advantage.

Troop Trains

New recruits arrived in New River on all-Women Marine trains carrying around 500 women, directed by a woman Lieutenant with two enlisted women assistants. One recruit commented: 'We started right out learning military procedure and discipline at the railroad station. The WRs lined us up, bag and baggage, and marched us aboard the train.'

On arrival at Camp Lejeune, boots observed the same strict rules applied to male recruits at Parris Island and San Diego boot camps. The whole day was programmed and no liberty was given during the six-week-long indoctrination. Women were assigned to billets in the red brick barracks of Area One, which were for the exclusive use of the women's schools. Training began immediately with orientation classes, issue of uniform, close-order drill the day after arrival, and classification tests and interviews for assessing abilities, education, training and business experience. Strict discipline applied, starting with getting up at 05.45, falling into formation at 06.30, breakfast at 06.45, then classes until 11.30, followed by a march to lunch and further classes or drill until 16.00. Military phraseology and customs also formed part of the training, although the story goes that one woman, upon passing an officer on the street, saluted and said, 'Leave me by sir', instead of, 'By your leave sir'. One student platoon leader, hesitating for a moment to ensure she gave the correct command, suddenly realised a tree was immediately ahead of them and called out, 'Around the tree . . . march!'

'Hometown' Platoons

An officer from the Southern Recruiting District raised a query one month after the forming of the Women's Reserve, asking, 'We are making plans for the formation of a platoon of Women Marines, to be sworn in jointly and sent to training as a group. This has been done successfully with male Marines in the past. If there is any objection to this, please wire immediately.' There was no objection from Headquarters.

Although this request appears to have come from Atlanta, the first WR platoon sent to camp was from Philadelphia, the birthplace of the Marine Corps in the days of the Revolution. This platoon arrived in September 1943, receiving a 'Welcome Aboard' telegram from Major Streeter. The first Pittsburgh platoon and the Potomac Platoon of Women Marines of Washington, DC, were all sworn in on the Marine Corps' 168th birthday. The Washington ceremony was held at the Library of Congress prior to the platoon leaving for Camp Lejeune, prompting one library official to remark: 'In all my years of association with the Library of Congress I have never seen the steps of the main building put to more appropriate use than the swearing in of the First Potomac Platoon of Women Marines.'

Other neighbourhood women's platoons were scheduled, including Albany, Buffalo (two), Northern New England, Pittsburgh (two), Miami, Alabama, Fayette County PA, Johnstown PA, St Paul, Green Bay, Westmoreland County PA, Seattle, Houston, Southern New England, Central New York and Dallas. Although members of the platoons were ordered to duty and underwent initial training as a unit, they were assigned individually to duty following training.

Aviation machinist

Motor Transport School (MTD)

Training at Camp Lejeune

The women Marines' training programme was designed to turn civilians into military personnel in the shortest possible time. As with their male counterparts, close-order drill proved to be an effective tool in proving the value of teamwork, military precision, instant reaction to command, discipline and order, pride in outfit and self, and the indefinable tradition of Marine *esprit*. On completion of their training, women were either immediately assigned to active duty or were referred to specialist schools or trained whilst apprentices in the job. Those with appropriate previous civilian skills were given supervisory roles.

Commanding Officers of the Camp Lejeune Women's Reserve were Lieutenant Colonel Lucian C. Whitaker, USMCR, and later John M. Arthur, USMC. Their command included the Recruit Depot, Candidates Class and Specialist Schools Detachment. Platoons in training had an average of 28 to 30 women, and a

Aerial gunnery school

company had approximately 165. In total, 22,199 women were sent to the recruit depots of Camp Lejeune and Hunter College, with only 602 failing to complete the course either for medical reasons or unsuitability.

Specialist Training
Over 100 members of the first class to graduate from Hunter attended Navy and Marine specialist schools. Navy courses were: Aviation Machinist Mate at the

Naval Training School, Memphis, Tennessee; Link Training Instructor at the Naval Air Station, Atlanta, Georgia, and Aviation Storekeeper at Indiana University, Bloomington, Indiana. Marine specialist schools included cooks and bakers, motor transport, quartermaster and non-commissioned officers. Members of the officer classes at Mount Holyoke were also offered further training including instruction at the Navy's communications school in South Hadley, Massachusetts. Before the end of the war, 30 specialist schools were available to women Marines and nearly 9,000 women took up advanced training. Courses varied in length from 4 to 22 weeks, and were available to women who had completed 'boot' training and qualified for higher ratings in specialist fields.

As well as the specialist schools, Marine Corps and Navy training was available on courses for first sergeant, paymaster, signal, parachute rigger, aerographer, clerical, control tower operator, aerial gunnery instructor, celestial navigation, motion picture operator's technician, aircraft instruments, radio operator, radio material, radio material teletypewriter, post exchange, uniform shop, aviation storekeeping, automotive mechanic, carburettor and ignition, aviation supply and photography. Several of the classes were also attended by veteran Marines whose experience was an added bonus.

Promotion from the Ranks

The first seven officer candidate classes consisted of women who enlisted in Class VI(a) directly from civilian life. Their applications were sent to Headquarters from the procurement district where they had enlisted. Applications for officer training were reviewed by a board of four in Washington, and the best qualified were ordered to duty. This was modified in July 1943 to allow enlisted women to apply for commissioned rank. The Commandant felt that this would provide opportunities for Class V(b) Reservists who,

> as a result of education, past experience and training, can supply the demand and perform the duties as officers. The plan of selecting commissioned personnel, in the main, from the ranks will build up a high standard of morale, efficiency and esprit de corps.

So, beginning with the eighth class in October 1943, the candidates class consisted of both civilian and enlisted women, the majority from the latter, who had to be recommended by their commanding officer. The review board for applications from enlisted personnel consisted of the Women's Reserve Director and regular and reserve male officers, who convened regularly to review and process applications. This new rule did not exclude civilian candidates, as those women with specialist abilities or who were considered to have outstanding leadership qualities were still accepted, however, this was far more limited. The first class of formerly enlisted Marines graduated on 15 December 1943, following which the majority of new women officers had served as enlisted before being commissioned.

Following the transfer to New River, all officer candidates were appointed to the rank of private first class for the entirety of the course. The same system was used in the men's Officer Candidates School (OCS) programme at Quantico. The category of cadet was dropped. Enlisted women holding the rank of Corporal or Sergeant temporarily reverted to Private First Class (PFC) and all candidates wore PFC chevrons and OC pins on uniform lapels and caps. Despite the appearance of equal rank the higher-ranked WRs were still paid at their substantive rank. Any enlisted woman who did not complete the course reverted to her rating but could re-apply 'without prejudice against her' in six months. Successful candidates were commissioned to the appropriate rank following completion of training – a small number of top candidates to first lieutenant and the remainder to second lieutenant. In some instances, particularly well-qualified candidates were awarded Captain but this was not an easy achievement, the dropout rate being over 30 per cent.

Reserve Officer Class
Although officer ranks were opened up to enlisted personnel in late 1943, it was soon found that even outstanding NCOs did not always make the transition to good officer and needed time to adjust whilst at school before going to their officer jobs. The first reserve officer class came in December after the eighth officer candidates' class. It comprised of successful graduates of officers' class, and graduates of earlier classes who had been on duty and for whom it was a refresher course. Emphasis was placed on personnel issues such as administration, recreation, messing, rehabilitation and the psychology of behaviour patterns that may be encountered on duty. This meant that the officer-training programme was extended to three months, including eight weeks of indoctrination and four weeks training by the reserve officer class.

OC pins

CHAPTER 2

JOBS AND JOB ASSIGNMENTS

All Marine Corps training for the women, both basic and specialist, was tough, the objective being to equip the Woman Marine to handle any day-to-day situation within her specialist field. Skill and precision were paramount, the slightest mistake potentially costing lives.

The 305 Women Marines of World War I (the so-called Marinettes) carried out primarily clerical work such as stenography, typing, bookkeeping and messaging. In contrast, the World War II USMCR women had a much wider range of jobs to choose from such as radio operator, photographer, parachute rigger, motor transport driver, aerial gunnery instructor, cook and baker, quartermaster, Link training instructor, control tower operator, motion picture technician, automotive mechanic, teletype operator, cryptographer, laundry manager and post exchange manager. There were also jobs in personnel management, stenography and related desk jobs. Despite the 1943 recruiting literature offering 'more than 30 different job assignments', the actual number was in excess of 200, covering some jobs previously considered to be male only and informal duties on some stations such as lifeguard in the swimming pool.

Job Classification
In March 1943 a job classification system was established to assist in matching women to jobs following completion of the indoctrination course. At the US Naval Training School in the Bronx and in the US Naval Reserve Midshipmen's School in Northampton, women reservists were asked about their professional experience, education, hobbies and knowledge of languages. The classification system came under the direction of Captain Cornelia Williams at Marine Corps Headquarters, who held a PhD in Psychology from the University of Minnesota and had wide experience as College Instructor and in student personnel work. The Women's Reserve section of the Detail Branch was responsible for classification and detail relating to Women Reservists, involving selection of tests, designing a qualification card, supervising the selection and training of classification personnel, and analysing jobs, giving them specification serial numbers. They planned the distribution of Women Marines to meet the needs of the service and requested the orders required to send them to schools or duty stations, matching the available billets to the available personnel.

Following the transfer of recruit training to Camp Lejeune, each Marine was tested and interviewed in the first week of training. The classification section at the Women's Reserve Schools determined eligibility for specialist schools and assignment to jobs. Classification specialists assigned to posts and stations assisted in the transfer of personnel to alternative posts as necessary.

Promotion
This proved a difficult area for enlisted personnel in the Women's Reserve, resulting

in 11 Letters of Instruction over two and a half years relating to various systems trialled. Finally, the system that appeared to work best was for 75 per cent of privates and privates first class to be ranked as private first class. Monthly quotas for promotion to 4th and 5th pay grades were allocated for each post, these being made by the post commander following successful outcome of testing. Promotions to the first three pay grades, however, were recommended by commanding officers and implemented by Marine Corps Headquarters as vacancies occurred.

For officers, promotion previously determined by seniority was later replaced by selection. Block promotion from second to first lieutenant was adopted and all Women's Reserve officers who had served in commissioned rank for at least 18 months were assured one promotion. Spot promotions were allowed where specialist skills were needed in a particular billet calling for a higher-ranking Marine. These promotions would become official when the woman qualified for regular promotion with those from the same training class, or equivalent seniority, and was selected for promotion to the next rank.

Jobs in Aviation

Before the end of the war, almost a third of Women Marines had served in aviation at Marine air commands and bases. The Division of Aviation had an existing special arrangement with the Marine Corps to allow it to train, assign and supervise its own personnel; this was extended to the women. Following recruit training, they took classification tests and were divided into two groups: one assigned to aviation and one to non-aviation. All personnel working in aviation – whether in technical assignments, or in administrative functions – were classified as holding aviation jobs. According to a 1943 memorandum, the key officer required for liaison and training duties would have aviation and business experience, plus the ability to work with the Division of Aviation on liaison, organisation, procurement and training. Since Marine and Naval Aviation were so closely linked, she should also have an understanding of both Navy Department and Marine Corps organisation. Marion B. Dryden and Katherine D. Lynch, of the 5th officers class and commissioned on 20 September 1943, were approved for appointment in the rank of Captain.

By 1944, all training in Link instruction was handled by Women Marines. They were almost completely in charge of the photography department and film library, 90% of parachute packing, inspecting and repairing, and 80% of landing field control tower operations. The large numbers of women on duty at Marine air stations resulted in a number of detachments being activated as Aviation Women's Reserve Squadrons, designed to supply technical and administrative personnel for the male Marine operational training unit. The Squadrons operation at the end of the war included:

Number 1 at Mojave
Number 2 at Santa Barbara
Number 3 at El Centro
Numbers 4 and 5 at Miramar
Numbers 6–10 at El Toro
Number 11 at Parris Island
Number 14 at Ewa, Hawaii
Numbers 15–20 at Cherry Point
Number 21 at Quantico

Below and opposite: Aviation mechanics

CHAPTER 3

ADMINISTRATION AND POLICIES

The original Plans and Policies study which had recommended forming a Women's Reserve, also suggested it be placed in the Adjutant and Inspector's Department, Division of Reserve, the latter being responsible for procurement of all Marine Corps reserve personnel. A new Women's Reserve Section unit was created, attached to the Division of Reserve, to deal with administration of the Women's Reserve, for example training, uniforming and regulations. A senior woman officer was assigned to major activities at Marine Corps Headquarters, which handled matters pertaining to the women such as Personnel, Administration, Public Information, Plans and Policies, and Supply.

At the time it was believed that women would be most useful to the Marine Corps if they were regarded as 'extra' Marines, therefore administrative action in respect of women was processed through arrangements already in place for the men, and the Women's Reserve was never organised as a separate unit.

The Director, MCWR, was charged with the 'procurement, instruction, training, discipline, organisation, administration and mobilisation of the Women's Reserve for the duration of the war and six months thereafter', and was attached to the Women's Reserve Section for 'purposes of instruction' from February to October 1943 as she became familiar with military procedures. In October she was transferred as Special Assistant to the Director of Personnel, her main duty being to advise him on policy concerning the Women's Reserve. The Director had considerable influence in developing policies and procedures for the Women's Reserve, but never actually took independent action on the administrative handling of the Reserve. She made recommendations to the Director of Personnel who was authorised to take action.

From an administrative point of view, the underlying tendency was to treat the Women Marines the same as any other Marines. Therefore, any regulations that could sensibly be shared were adopted for the Women and in some cases for the WAVES, since initial recruitment and training of the Women Marines had been in conjunction with the WAVES. Experience was shared between the various women's services, including the Canadian Women's Army Corps, to whom Lieutenant Colonel John B. Hill, USMC, had paid a visit in January 1943, prior to the formation of the Marine Corps Women's Reserve, to learn about curricula, personnel policies and any other details which may be helpful in forming the new service.

Cooperation with the Women's Services
Although the women's services were competitive in their eagerness to enlist well-qualified candidates, they were at the same time cooperative with the other services, their respective leaders being:

Colonel Oveta Culp Hobby, WAAC and WAC
Captain Mildred H McAfee, WAVES
Captain Dorothy C Stratton, SPARS

An example of the four leaders working together was in drawing up a unified programme of recruiting and enlistment of women from the war industries, civil service and agriculture. Once they were agreed, their recommendation was submitted to the Joint Army-Navy Personnel Board who in turn issued the policy to be followed by all four women's reserves. The enlistment of women employed by the war industries was discouraged and release from those industries was by reference to the United States Employment Service. Civil service women who wished to enlist in the Marine Reserve must first obtain written release from the agency. Those released 'without prejudice' could apply to the Women's Reserve on the same conditions as a non-civil service employee. However, if a resignation was accepted 'with prejudice' and the employer was reluctant to release the woman, she was ineligible for the armed services until 90 days after resignation. Civil service employees resigning to enlist in the Marines were not returned to their former place of work, even if their military job classification was identical to their civilian occupation.

The Marine Corps held a three-day open house at Camp Lejeune from 13 to 15 October 1943, following the transfer of all women's training activities. This event was planned to inform all women's services and included inspection of training facilities and methods, and observing Women Marines at work. The WACs, WAVES and SPARS were all represented, in addition to several high-ranking male officers from the corresponding services.

Policy about Assignment and Housing
The Marine Corps had decided that Women Marines would be assigned 'only to posts where their services have been requested'. The provision of housing in connection with these assignments was an obvious consideration and had arisen in the November 1942 Plans and Policies survey, which had sought to determine numbers required by various posts and the quarters available for them. Women were not to be assigned to posts unless proper housing or quarters with the WAVES could be provided.

In addition, policy decreed that no less than two women would be assigned to a station or sub-station to 'prevent loneliness and obviate possible unfavourable comment'. Enlisted women were not to be assigned to a post unless a woman officer was present or nearby, however, it became a general rule that women officers were not assigned to units of fewer than 25 women, the exception being assignment to procurement offices in large cities. The projected ratio of officers to enlisted was 5.7%.

On completion of training, women were assigned to duty on posts and stations under the commanding officer of their unit, reporting in turn to the commanding officer of the post. The Women Marines had relative autonomy in relation to quarters, mess facilities and administration, and those living on the regular posts had their own barracks area that they maintained. Where MCWR personnel were stationed in cities and were few in number, the women were allocated a subsistence allowance; for higher numbers such as for the 2,400 in Washington, DC, Henderson Hall was built and operated as an independent post. It was found that in barracks situations, living as a military unit, the health, feeding, military behaviour and discipline were improved, as the women enjoyed a comradeship and felt more like Marines than those who were more isolated.

More often than not, the women's work was supervised by a male officer, but everyday discipline and command issues were left to the Women's Reserve officer. This sharing of command seemed to work well in practice.

Assistants for the Women's Reserve

In the fall of 1943, several thousand of the Women's Reserve found themselves assigned to more widely spread posts across the country, and it was now imperative to develop a regular reporting system to keep Marine Corps Headquarters fully informed, whether by official correspondence, Director's field visits or by word of mouth. The most senior woman officer of any station where Women Marines were serving was therefore designated 'Assistant for the Women's Reserves' and was responsible for advising the Director on welfare, jobs, health, training, housing, recreation and discipline. The Assistant for Women's Reserve was also responsible for keeping the commanding officer of the post informed on all issues relating to the women within his authority.

When the system of monthly reporting was introduced, the Assistant for the Women's Reserve prepared this for Marine Corps Headquarters and copied it to the post commanding officer, detailing any aspect of the women's jobs, well-being and any 'items of special interest at the station'. These reports were in addition to the visits of the Director, who had allocated 25% of her time to be spent on visits to observe the operation of Women's Reserve units throughout the country.

Policy about Women's Authority

Women officers' authority was 'over women of the Reserve only' and was 'limited to the administration of the Women's Reserve'. The relationship of women officers or non-commissioned officers to enlisted men had been likened to that of a civilian teacher in a military school and it was decreed that whilst the woman officer could give instructions regarding the work, any disciplinary issues 'should be referred to the man's commanding officer'. The authority of women officers did cause some confusion when differentiating between matters of discipline and matters of job performance, to the extent that the Commandant felt it necessary to clarify:

> It appears that the services of officers and non-commissioned officers of the Marine Corps Women's Reserve are not being utilised to the fullest extent due to some doubt as to the scope of their authority. This matter has been considered by the Navy department and it is concluded that it is entirely proper for a woman officer to be assigned to duty subordinate to a commanding officer and her directions and orders in the proper performance of such duty are the acts of the officer in command, even though such orders are directed to male personnel.

This opened the door for Women Marine officers to be assigned the duties of Adjutant, Assistant Adjutant, Personnel Officer or Mess Officer, 'where the directions and orders necessary in the performance of such duties [were] considered as emanating from the commanding officer'.

Changing Policy on Marriage
When recruiting started in February 1943 an applicant could be either single or married, as long as her children were not under-18 and she was not married to a Marine. This rule was issued by the Secretary of Navy and applied to WAVES, SPARS and Marines, all of who could not be enlisted or appointed if their husbands were in the same service. Also, members of the Naval Reserve could not, 'while in service, marry an officer or enlisted man in the same service'.

An amendment to this rule was made in March 1943, allowing a member of the Naval Reserve to marry after she entered the service, however not 'during the period of their indoctrination or training'. The Marine Corps interpreted this period to be basic training (boot or candidates' school) rather than the entire period of training, which often included a month at specialist school. Indoctrination was six weeks, during which the women learned 'the principles of military life' and following which their commitments 'must be secondary to their obligation to the Marine Corps'. Also, specialist schools could last as long as four months, and, as men were being sent overseas in great numbers the marriage may not have happened at all.

Late in 1943, wives of Marines 'below the rank of second lieutenant' were allowed to enlist. However, having disagreed with the WAVES at the time this was discussed, the Marine Corps emphasised: 'Each wife shall be made to understand that the probability of being stationed with her husband is very slight and that consideration cannot be given to personal desires in the matter.'

Wedding of 'Manila John' Basilone, first Enlisted Marine recipient of the Medal of Honor in World War II, KIA Iwo Jima, 1945.

CHAPTER 4

SPECIALIST UNITS AND DECORATIONS

The Women's Reserve Band

The band was initially allowed 43 women and was formed at Camp Lejeune with the aim of becoming 'the most outstanding female band of the country'. To this end, the Marine Corps wrote to several prominent music schools and colleges informing them of the band and asking them to make recommendations of suitable candidates. This resulted in many women applying for the band before enlistment and joining the service for the sole purpose of becoming a member of the band. Women who were already in the Reserve could also try out for the band and were accepted into it if considered to be suitably talented. Members were carefully screened and auditioned before being selected.

Captain William F. H. Santelmann organised the band in November 1943, and training was provided by the US Marine Band. The Director was Master Sergeant Charlotte Plummer who had been director of music in the Portland, Oregon public school system prior to her enlistment, in addition to being a member of the city's municipal band. The band was based at Camp Lejeune and played at the Saturday morning MCWR Recruit Depot reviews. They also played on every Marine Base on the east coast and toured widely, playing in front of many distinguished people, including President Franklin D. Roosevelt, Admiral Chester W. Nimitz, and, in October 1945, on a tour in Washington for the Nimitz

WR band

WR band

Day parade, played for the Commandant, General Alexander A. Vandegrift, outside his office in the Navy Annex.

The US Treasury requested them to take part in the war bond and victory loan events. The theme song, 'March of the Women Marines', was composed especially for the band by Master Sergeant Louis Saverino and Technical Sergeant Emil Grasser.

Quantico's Drill Team
Women Marines upheld the Corps' reputation for excellence in drill in their trick drill platoon of the Women's Reserve Battalion, Marine Corps Base, Quantico, giving special performances for visiting dignitaries and appearing at social and military functions. The team was set up in 1944 and commended by Brigadier Archie R. Howard, noting that the excellence of this team's work 'has been attained by personal sacrifice of many liberty hours, in as much as all time devoted to instruction has been entirely voluntary and in addition to regular assignments.'

Decorations Awarded to Women Marines
The highest award given to a Woman Marine as a result of service in World War II was the Legion of Merit, awarded to two wartime Directors, Colonel Ruth Cheney Streeter and Colonel Katherine A. Towle. Majors Helen N. Crean and Marion Wing received the Bronze Star Medal. Letters of commendation and Commendation Medals were presented to more than 30 enlisted women and officers of the Women's Reserve. Resulting from World War II service, Women Marines were eligible to wear the Good Conduct Medal, American Campaign Medal, World War II Victory Medal and Asiatic-Pacific Campaign Medal.

CHAPTER 5

HAWAII DUTY

According to widespread 'scuttlebutt' in summer 1944, there was a possibility that Women Marines would be sent overseas for the first time. Congress had been debating this for over a year, which would necessitate amending the Naval Reserve Act of 1938 to allow women in the naval service to serve outside the continental limits of the United States. Initial objection in the House now seemed to have turned into favourable action by the Senate, encouraged by the Senate Naval Affairs Committee on its companion bill. To date there had been no official word that Women Marines would be placed in overseas billets such as Pearl Harbor to release the men for combat, however, informal mention had been made by officers back from the Pacific, including General Holland M. Smith. Secretary of the Navy James V. Forrestal had told Congress that approximately 5,000 naval servicewomen would be required immediately in Hawaii alone.

On 13 September the Senate passed the bill subsequently adopted by the House and signed into law by the President on 27 September 1944. This Public Law 441, 78th Congress, modified the existing Department of Navy Regulations, permitting 'female Naval personnel to serve on a volunteer basis anywhere within the western hemisphere, including Alaska and Hawaii'.

The Women's Reserve Director had anticipated specific problems that may arise when the announcement was made to send women overseas, and had previously submitted draft policies for personnel selection in preparation for authorisation of overseas service. The Marine Corps did consider sending one group of women to Pearl Harbor to form the Women's Reserve Battalion, attached to Marine Garrison Forces, and a small detachment to the Marine Air Station at Ewa. Colonel Streeter and Major Marion B. Dryden, senior Women's Reserve personnel officer in the Division of Aviation, carried out a fact-finding mission on 13 October. They flew to Hawaii, inspected the area, spoke with Marine and Navy officers on the job categories of the men to be released for combat, asked what quarters would be available for women or could be converted for them, and examined the existing chain of command, recreation facilities, regulations and procedures for service personnel on the island and other related matters. When they returned, they recommended two detachments of Women Marines as was originally planned. Although these two units would be administered separately by their own women commanding officers, both would ultimately be under the final jurisdiction of the 14th Naval District.

Selection of Women for Overseas Duty
Every woman who volunteered for Hawaii duty was screened and selection was based partly on length of service in the Marine Corps, however, it was primarily based on the job classifications of the men to be released. These included clerical, communications, quartermaster, telephone operator, mechanical, motor transport and

radio operator. The group chosen included some women whose brothers had been killed in action or had been taken prisoner of war and some who had relatives still fighting on the front. Responsibility, maturity, adaptability and emotional stability were considered to be the main personal characteristics required. Other necessary qualifications were at least six months' service on active duty (excluding training time); good health, conduct and work records; and being free from any dependency which may require them to be present at home. Overseas duty was for a two-year period and leave to return to the States was authorised for emergency only.

The wording of the legislation meant that a woman naval reservist had to volunteer for overseas duty and could not be ordered into it. Careful consideration had to be given to the applications received to establish the motivation for volunteering and perceived 'glamour' was dispelled by the Marine Corps. Brigadier General Waller, Commanding General, Marine Garrison Forces in Hawaii, stated in a memorandum:

> All WRs should be informed this duty here is not glamorous – just hard work. They will be under more restrictions than at home, and their working and living conditions may not be as good . . . they will be closer to the war, they will see ships damaged in combat, and they will see and meet many men who have recently been in combat.

The Canadian Women's Army Corps had recommended that a volunteer should be able to 'maintain good adjustment when her work is dull or monotonous or when she has to work under pressure or conditions of strain.' This became a consideration, particularly taking into account the Hawaii operation, which necessitated seven-day working. Although half-day or full-day liberty was programmed in each week, when it became necessary, round-the-clock working was in operation until the priority job was complete.

Advance Party
An advance party flew to Hawaii on 2 December to make arrangements for the reception of the battalion of approximately 100 housekeeping personnel and the Women Marines who would follow, numbering around 1,000. The advance party consisted of Major Marion Wing, one of the original 19 former WAVES, who was assigned as Commanding Officer at Pearl Harbor; First Lieutenant Dorothy C. McGinnis, who was Adjutant at Pearl Harbor; First Lieutenant Ruby V. Bishop, the Battalion Quartermaster; and Second Lieutenant Pearl M. Martin, Recreation Officer.

The advance party for the aviation unit followed, consisting of Captain Helen N. Crean, the Commanding Officer at Ewa; First Lieutenant Caroline J. Ransom, the Post Exchange Officer; Second Lieutenant Constance M. Berkolz, the Pearl Harbor Mess Officer; and Second Lieutenant Bertha K. Ballard, Mess Officer at Ewa.

Staging Area and Arrival in Hawaii
The first volunteers for overseas duty were transferred in January 1945 to a staging area at Marine Corps Base, San Diego, California. They were given a short intensive physical conditioning course, including qualification swimming, drill and

calisthenics. They also learned to ascend and descend the cargo net of a ship mock-up carrying full 10-pound packs on their backs, and how to jump into the water from shipboard in case they met with an enemy attack whilst en route to their destination. They were given physical examinations, inoculations, a review of Marine Corps administration and organisation, inspection of uniforms and gear,

Destination Hawaii

lectures about the people of Hawaii, Allied insignia, safeguarding of military information, procedures on board ship and a final screening.

On 25 January, 160 enlisted and five WR officers, dressed in winter greens and trench coats, and carrying blanket rolls, sailed from San Francisco on board the SS *Matsonia*. The women marched on board in column and into assigned quarters. After two days at sea they changed into work/utility uniforms – sage green short-sleeve utility shirt, HBT slacks and garrison cap. This would become the uniform of the day for the duration of their Hawaiin cruise. The women staged their own entertainment show whilst on board and maintained standards in their own area. The *Matsonia* arrived in Honolulu on 28 January, the women being led ashore, dressed in Forest Greens, by Captain Marna V. Brady, Officer-in-Charge of the voyage, assigned Battalion Executive Officer. She was met with the customary Hawaiian lei and kiss.

One Woman Marine, Corporal Alice M. Philpotts, had travelled to the States from her home in Honolulu, a few miles from Pearl Harbor, to enlist in the Marines. Corporal Philpotts had been in Pearl Harbor on the day of the December 1941 attack.

Crowds had assembled at the dockside, and the women were cheered by residents, civilian war workers and servicemen alike. There were colourful leis, flashes from the cameras of photographers and surprise on the expressions of male Marines who had never seen a Woman Marine before. The Pearl Harbor Marine Barracks band played the soft music of the traditional Aloha 'Oe and the military tunes of the Marine Hymn and March of the Women Marines. The majority of the women were housed in the Moanalua Ridge area where the Women's Reserve Battalion occupied a former Seabee area adjacent to the Marine Corps Sixth Base Depot and Camp Catlin. The air group were assigned to the nearby Marine Air Station at Ewa.

Women Marines drew not only the surprise of the male Marines, but smiles

WR Boxing 'Smoker' en route to Hawaii

Dungarees and field coats were the uniform of the day for all WRs en-route to Hawaii

HAWAII DUTY

Arrival in Hawaii

and waves from the local people and, on their first visit to the mess hall, from a small dog who growled at this unusual sight, until commanded by a messman, 'Knock it off, Taffy, after all they're Marines too'.

In Hawaii, as in the States, the Women Marines took the place of men in office jobs and in specialised work, standing night watches in communications and various other duty assignments, and working the same hours as the men. At Pearl Harbor, the women ran the entire motor transport, which provided service for around 16,000 people each month and included liberty buses, work detail trucks and jeeps. Thirty-three vehicles in total were operated, working 24 hours a day and with a perfect safety record.

Women Marines assigned to the air station found that conditions were very similar to mainland air stations; more than a third of them had previously been stationed at Cherry Point.

Additional detachments arrived each week from the States, approximately 200 enlisted women and 10 officers on each occasion. By the time the fourth of these groups arrived, the WR Battalion was organised. Shrubs, trees and plants had appeared as if overnight, the Seabees had done renovation work on the administration building, barracks, mess hall and laundry, and the women had joined in with the landscaping and assisting the Seabees. One male Marine was heard to exclaim, 'The Army has its WACs, the Navy its WAVES, the Coast Guard its SPARS and the Seabees OUR Marines.'

The women were in great demand for social events, to the extent that an enlisted women's council had to screen the incoming requests and decide, on behalf of all WRs, which they could attend. Several 'air hops' were arranged to allow women to visit the Marine detachments on the islands of Hawaii and Maui. In May 1945, the first all-Marine overseas weddings was held between Sergeant

WR colour guard – Pearl Harbor

Dorothy Jeanne Crane, a photographer on duty with the Marine Garrison Forces and Staff Sergeant Robert T. Davis. Whilst the bride had the traditional white gown, her tiara was of white orchids and she carried pikake leis in her bouquet. The majority of the guests were Marines, both male and female, however, one of the civilian guests was Representative Margaret Chase Smith, the only woman member of the House Naval Affairs Committee, who had helped to draft the legislation for the overseas bill and was, at the time, in Hawaii on an investigative tour. Probably the most notable of all Marine weddings was between Sgt Lena Mae Riggi and Gunnery Sgt John Basilone, awarded the Medal of Honour on Guadalcanal and after war bond tours assigned to the 5th Marine Division. He was killed in action on Iwo Jima in February 1945.

Approximately 1,000 women saw duty with the Marine Garrison Forces at Pearl Harbor and the Marine Corps Air Station at Ewa, the announcement of VJ day in September 1945 bringing their two-year duty to a halt. The first women left Hawaii in December 1945, the remainder following in January.

Welcome Luau

CHAPTER 6

DEMOBILISATION

'War is over'

Following the cessation of hostilities and the announcement of VJ day, all recruiting for the Women's Reserve ceased, although those in training stayed until completion and were then assigned to duty. Recruitment had been slowed down since the summer of 1944, when the Marine Corps had reached its target of 18,000 enlisted and 1,000 officers, so the number still in training was quite small and was to cover natural replacement. The 'Adjusted Service Rating System', similar to the one used for the men, was employed to progress the demobilisation, and women were given the same discharge credits as their male counterparts. However, women could only earn credits by length of service, as the categories of combat or dependent children did not apply to them, therefore the number of credits required for discharge was lowered to 25, rather than 85 for men.

The closure date for the Women's Reserve was originally 1 September 1946, by which time all women were to be discharged. This was confirmed in the Headquarters Marine Corps bulletin, Commandant Lieutenant General A. A. Vandegrift adding the words:

> It was with some hesitation that the Marine Corps admitted women to its ranks in February 1943, but during the intervening years they have made a most valuable contribution to the Corps . . . As the time comes to release them I am reminded again of the important part they have played in support of our combat Marines while the actual fighting was in progress . . . I wish

to express to the members of the Women's Reserve the appreciation of the Marine Corps for the valuable contribution they have made for its success. They have performed their duties in a manner that evokes the admiration and praise of their fellow Marines, and their conduct and appearance, both on and off duty, have been exemplary and a source of pride to us all.

A two-week 'Rehabilitation School' was set up at Headquarters and at Camp Lejeune for Women Reserve officers and non-commissioned officers. Information was available on rights and benefits under the Veterans Administration and GI Bill of Rights for the women who were being discharged into civilian life. Letters of recommendation were written for former and prospective employers, and credit requests were made to high schools on the basis of the recruit training and experience gained in the Women's Reserve. Information was also gained from Colleges on their entrance requirements. A group of women who were being discharged listed their future plans as new employment, education, old employment, housewife and civil service.

In November 1945 some newspapers quoted the Commandant as saying that the Marine Corps Women's Reserve would be reduced from 18,000 enlisted to 2,638 and from 1,000 officers to 200 by June 1946. They further quoted him as saying that the organisation would 'completely vanish from the picture by September of next year'. In fact, the MCWR was reduced to two thirds of its strength by 7 December 1945. The original Director, Colonel Streeter, having been promoted to Lieutenant Colonel on 22 November 1943 and to Colonel on 1 February 1944, resigned to be at home for her three sons, who were all returning from overseas duty. Lieutenant Katherine A. Towle of Berkeley, California, succeeded her, assuming the Directorship and its rank of Colonel on 7 December 1945.

In addition, the Women's Reserve band was officially disbanded at Camp Lejeune on 28 November 1945 when 26 of its members were discharged under the credit provisions of Letter of Instruction 1110; the remaining 21 being reassigned in the Women's Reserve Battalion. Each member of the band was presented with a gold bracelet with her name and the inscription 'Thanks from Camp Lejeune'.

Lieutenant General Vandegrift

Director Katherine Towle, USMCWR

Strength at End of the War

Two and a half years after the Marine Corps Women's Reserve was formed there were approximately 17,640 women and 820 officers on duty, a total of 18,460. There were 28 units headed by women commanding officers and 17 smaller units. Women were also assigned to specialist duties such as recruiting.

Line units included Women's Reserve Battalions at Henderson Hall Quantico, Camp Lejeune, Parris Island, San Diego, Camp Pendleton and Pearl Harbor, the School Detachment at Camp Lejeune. Women Marine companies were at San Diego; Department of the Pacific, San Francisco; the Navy Yard at Mare Island, California; and Washington, DC. Aviation units included Cherry Point, Quantico, Parris Island, El Toro, Miramar, El Centro, Santa Barbara, Mojave, Ewa Hawaii and Eagle Mountain Lake, Texas. The four Quartermaster units to which Women Marines were assigned were Depot of Supplies in Philadelphia; South Annex, Norfolk; Camp Elliott, California: and Depot of Supplies, San Francisco. Women were also stationed at the four procurement districts:

Eastern at Philadelphia
Southern in Atlanta
Central in Chicago
Western at San Francisco.

Last Days of the Wartime Reserve

Women's Reserve activity had been disbanded at Camp Lejeune (Women's Reserve Battalion), Parris Island and the Depot of Supplies, Philadelphia, by 2 June 1946. By 1 July, WR units were deactivated at Quantico, Camp Lejeune (Women's Reserve Separation Centre), Camp Pendleton and Marine Corps Air Depot Miramar. The only Women's Reserve units remaining until the 1 September terminating date were at Henderson Hall and Cherry Point on the east coast and El Toro and Department of the Pacific, San Francisco on the west. With a few exceptions, the remaining Women Reservists on duty from 1 July to 1 September were volunteers. The organisation had been reduced to approximately 1,000 by 1 July, this number being gradually decreased in the final two months, when the majority of Women Marines still in uniform were stationed at Henderson Hall, whilst on duty at Marine Corps Headquarters.

Colonel Towle, on termination of the office of Director of the Women's Reserve on 14 June 1946, before she returned to civilian life, commented:

> General morale during demobilisation has been gratifyingly high. Part of this has been due to the definite stand the Marine Corps itself has taken, from the beginning, on the Marine Corps Women's Reserve demobilisation, particularly in setting and maintaining 1 September 1946 as the terminal date of the wartime Women's Reserve. It has been a goal to work toward and Marine Corps women have never had the uncertainty and confusion concerning demobilisation which have occurred in some of the other women's services because of the shifting of dates and changes in policy.

CHRONOLOGY – US MARINE CORPS WOMEN'S RESERVE

1942

31 October 1942   Secretary of the Navy, Frank Knox, authorizes Marine Corps to create a Women's Reserve and to accept women applicants for commissions and enlistments.

7 November 1942   Approval by Commandant, Lieutenant General Thomas Holcomb, of formation of Marine Corps Women's Reserve.

1943

29 January 1943   Commissioning of Major Ruth Cheney Streeter as Director, Marine Corps Women's Reserve.

13 February 1943   First day that enlistment officially opens.

13 March 1943   First class of 71 officer candidates enters US Naval Midshipmen's School (WR) at Mount Holyoke, Massachusetts, to begin training with the WAVES.

26 March 1943   First class of enlisted Women's Reserves, numbering 722, begins training at the JS Navel Training School (WR) at Hunter College, the Bronx, New York; likewise training with the WAVES.

25 April 1943   First class of enlisted women graduates and are assigned to active duty. Subsequent classes of approximately 525 women enter every two weeks for courses averaging about four weeks in length.

4 May 1943   First class of officer candidates graduate and report to duty stations. Classes averaging about 70 candidates and lasting about eight weeks began every month.

15 July 1943   Training for enlisted and candidates having been transferred to Camp Lejeune, North Carolina, during past week, instruction for both groups commences here this date. All basic training for Women's Reserves, as well as much of the speciality training, is held here throughout the rest of the war.

20 October 1943	First candidates class, i.e. the eighth, composed of meritorious enlisted women, begins its training; OCC thereafter comprises largely of former enlisted women.

1944
13 February 1944	First Anniversary of Women's Reserve finds organization having grown from four women to nearly 15,000 and is well within sight of its recruiting goal: a strength of 18,000 enlisted and 1,000 officers. Original prediction of 'more than 30 kinds of jobs' grows to more than 200 different assignments.
27 September 1944	Overseas Bill for women in the naval services is signed by the President; this allows women naval reservists to serve as volunteers anywhere within western hemisphere, including Hawaii and Alaska.

1945
29 January 1945	First detachment of five MCWR officers and 160 enlisted women arrives in Hawaii for overseas assignment. Later groups of approximately 200 arrive every other week. The Hawaii complement eventually totalled approximately 1,000 women.
13 February 1945	Second anniversary of Women Reserves is celebrated with dances, birthday cakes, special religious services and battalion reviews. The women number from one third to one half of the post troops at many Marine duty stations.
7 May 1945	VE Day. All recruiting for Women's Reserve limited to replacements for normal attrition.

1946–1948
13 February 1946	Some 17,999 Women Reserves are marched smartly in review before Commandant, General Alexander A. Vandegrift, in ceremonies at Washington, DC marking the third anniversary of the Women's Reserve.
7 June 1946	Approval by the Commandant of Marine Corps Women's Reserve Policy Board recommendation for retention of small number of women on duty to serve as trained nucleus for possible mobilization emergencies.
1 September 1946	Original terminal date set for Women's Reserve. All WR units disbanded and most of women return to civilian life.

12 June 1948 Passage of Women's Armed Services Integration Act establishes Women Marines as a permanent part of regular component of Marine Corps, as well as permanent reserve status.

4 November 1948 First group of three wartime WR officers sworn into the regular Marine Corps.

10 November 1948 First group of eight World War II enlisted women similarly sworn into the regular Marine Corps by the Commandant.

2275-45
DB-311-rwg

HEADQUARTERS U.S. MARINE CORPS
WASHINGTON

16 July, 1943

LETTER OF INSTRUCTION NO. 489

From: The Commandant, U.S. Marine Corps.
To: All Commanding Officer, Posts and Stations within the United States.
All Officers, Marine Corps Women's Reserve
Subject: Marine Corps Women's Reserve: Official observances; appearances in public; and marital status.

1. The program under which the Marine Corps Women's Reserve has become an integral part of the Marine Corps is well under way and; the Commandant takes this opportunity to express his welcome to those new members and to commend both officers and enlisted personnel for the manner and spirit in which they have entered upon and performed the duties to which they have been assigned.

2. The wide-spread interest reflected in Congress and through the press strongly indicates that the future existence of this branch of the Marine Corps depends largely upon the reaction of the American public to the demeanor of its members. It is felt that in this respect the Women's Reserve will continue to hold the position of high esteem which it deserves only if the utmost care is exercised in deportment, manner, and appearance of its individual members.

3. Uniform instructions will be issued at an early date. In addition certain rules of conduct will be published from time to time supplementing those herein prescribed. The following will be observed and followed:

(a) Saluting of and by the Marine Corps Women's Reserve shall be governed in general, by the same regulations and customs applicable to the Marine Corps. Junior salute first, whether it be a junior man saluting a woman Marine, or a junior woman saluting a senior man. Indoors under conditions where men are customarily uncovered (theatre, church, meals, etc.) members of the Marine Corps Women's Reserve will not salute even though covered. Under these conditions it is considered that the cap is worn, not as a badge of office, but in conformance to civilian rather than military custom.

(b) Officers shall be addressed by their rank. Instead of "sir", "ma'am" may be used when addressing an officer of the Marine Corps Women's Reserve.

(c) The rules of military courtesy apply - rank takes precedence. But because military courtesy includes deference to women, if a senior man officer indicates he prefers this courtesy above strict military usage, the junior woman should act accordingly without any hesitation or embarrassing counter-deference.

(d) The question will arise of women Marine officers attending social functions with enlisted personnel of both sexes, or enlisted women attending with officers of both sexes. The custom of the service requires great circumspection in social relationships in order to avoid any compromising of their relative military position, and members of the Marine Corps Women's Reserve shall observe the established custom whereby commissioned officers and enlisted personnel do not associate socially.

(e) Calling cards, if used, shall be in ladies' size, engraved in accordance with Marine Corps custom. Calls on commanding officers shall be made at the office if they are bachelors.

(f) Smoking shall be permitted as in civilian life, except on the street and in areas where prohibited by commanding officers.

(g) Drinking on duty is prohibited. Drinking off duty is permissible but if carried to excess is punishable according to the articles for the government of the Navy. Possession of liquor by enlisted personnel in billets is prohibited.

(h) Lipstick, if worn, shall be the same color as cap cord, winter service, and shall be neatly and thinly applied. Rouge, if worn, shall be inconspicuous. Colored nail polish, if worn, shall harmonize with color of winter service cap cord and lipstick. Mascara shall not be worn.

4. Members of the Marine Corps Women's Reserve who marry will immediately inform this Headquarters. Husbands full name and address will be given in order that records may be brought up to date. If a change of name is desired request for such change shall be made. Women reservists desiring to retain their maiden name should so indicate.

5. Commanding officers will furnish a copy of this letter to each enlisted member of the Marine Corps Women's Reserve.

T. HOLCOMB

Letter of Instruction – Uniforms

THE UNIFORMS

The basic ensemble of uniforms for the WRs was already in place months before the announcement of the formation of the Marine Corps Women's Reserve in February of 1943. In mid-December 1942, a memorandum from the Marine Commandant to the Assistant Secretary of the Navy requested that Mrs Anne Adams Lentz, then an employee of the War Department, be assigned to duty at Marine Headquarters for a period of approximately 30 days to assist in the design of the various uniforms intended for the forthcoming Women's Reserves, USMC.

Mrs Lentz had previously been employed by the school uniforms section of a large New York department store, before assisting the uniform board of the US Army for the Army Women's Auxiliary Army Corps (WAAC) uniforms. Mrs Lentz reported for duty in early January 1943 and, after consultation with the Marine Depot Quartermaster in Philadelphia, was dispatched to New York City to oversee construction of the various WR uniform samples by the Women's Garment Manufacturers of New York. These samples were subsequently shown to and approved by the Marine Commandant.

Before Mrs Lentz's 30-day assignment expired, she requested to enlist in the forthcoming Women's Reserve, USMC. She was accepted, becoming the first Woman Marine Reservist, and was sworn in as Captain Lentz, USMC, on 15 January 1943, the oath of office being administered by Brigadier General John M. Lentz, US Army – her husband!

Initially, WR uniforms were manufactured by various civilian firms under contract with the Marine Quartermaster. These firms sold the uniform items to various outlets (with a 10% profit margin), which subsequently sold the uniforms to the individual Woman Marine (with a 30% profit margin). Women Marines were given an allowance of $250 for Officers and $200 for Enlisted and were required to purchase the various uniform items prior to reporting for induction and training (see mimeograph to Lillian Sandy, Appendix 4).

This system of procurement of uniforms was flawed from the outset and uniform shortages became critical, many WRs doing their induction and training wearing part uniform items along with civilian dress. In June 1943 the Uniform Unit, Women's Reserve Section and the Quartermaster General, USMC were assigned

Captain Anne A. Lentz

responsibilities with respect to the design of garments, tariff of sizes, estimates of requirements and authorisation of retail outlets. The Philadelphia Depot was further responsible for the procurement of samples, preparation of specifications, stocking and furnishing of required materials and making necessary plans and negotiation for procurement of finished garments. Furthermore, in an effort to overcome difficulties in fitting uniforms at posts and stations, 13 WR officers were attached to Marine Headquarters in Washington from September through to December 1943 for training in the various phases of tailoring, alterations and fitting, these 13 WR officers being transferred to various posts and stations to be assigned to uniform shops operated by the Post Exchanges (PX).

Difficulties persisted in the manufacture and distribution of Women's Reserve clothing and it was finally decided that the system under which these procedures were handled was unworkable. A recommendation was made to the Quartermaster General of the Marine Corps that his office take over Women's Reserve clothing. In a letter dated 10 February 1944, the Quartermaster General proposed that his office arrange procurement and distribution of Women's Reserve clothing and accessories, and recommended that the Uniform Unit of the Women's Reserve Section, together with all uniform functions handled by that Unit, be transferred to the Office of the Quartermaster General, who would then be authorised to expend funds for the procurement of the necessary quantities of clothing. This letter was approved by the Commandant of the Marine Corps, and, on 16 February 1944, the Uniform Unit of the Women's Reserve Section, Reserve Division, Procurement Branch, was transferred to the Office of the Quartermaster General and became the Women's Reserve Section, Supply Division, Quartermaster Department.

The Women's Reserve Section immediately took steps to put in place the following with effect from 1 September 1944:

(a) Termination of all agreements with retail outlets and transfer of existing post exchange function in respect of uniforms and accessories to the Quartermaster
(b) Estimate and procure uniform and accessories requirements for one and a half years
(c) Establish a supply depot for Women's Reserve clothing and accessories at Richmond, Virginia
(d) Plan for maintenance of preferred stock levels, taking into account past sales and issues, and making provision for replenishing stock on the basis of the stock levels set up for Women's Reserve clothing. When stocks of each item held at the Richmond depot reached a designated stock level, material was to be ordered to allow adequate time for the contractor to begin manufacture and maintain appropriate stock levels
(e) Revise tariffs of sizes as necessary. Commercial tariffs were not suitable and sizes often changed after the recruit left the training school at Camp Lejeune. If difficulty existed in preparing a tariff of men's sizes, then this was even more so for women's sizes. There are records of sizing tariffs evolving from July 1943, when the Uniform Unit was given the first physical standard for Women's Reserve personnel, based on the record cards of 1,500 Women Reservists. Since then, a continual development was carried out, revisions being made on

physical standards, surveys from posts and stations to determine sizes of garments worn and information from the Uniform Shop at Camp Lejeune.

In August 1944, four Women's Reserve Officers were assigned to the Women's Reserve Section as inspectors, their duties to include making inspections at the premises of the various contracted manufacturers, maintaining liaison with them and progressing to completion the various contracts. The establishment of this service proved to have considerable value in procurement of the original stocks of Women's Reserve uniforms, the replenishment of this stock and the design and procurement of new articles of uniform.

After setting up the system of procurement and distribution of uniforms, attention turned to improvement in design and workmanship of uniforms and work garments. In October 1944, the Women's Reserve Section took over the preparation of all specifications and drawings for Women's Reserve garments, including production of standard samples for each authorised item of uniform. The Philadelphia Depot of Supplies was responsible for writing all specifications until the Women's Reserve Section took over this duty. In this instance, the Philadelphia Depot based their requirements on experience of writing specifications for men's clothing. This of course proved to be inadequate due to the different characteristics in women's clothing. Specifications were sent to the Women's Reserve Section for approval and returned to the Philadelphia Depot with recommended changes, which were corrected by the Depot. They were then re-submitted to Headquarters for approval. This process created obvious delays to final acceptance of the specification. When manufacturers suggested improvements to a garment, it could not be approved until the Philadelphia Depot had been notified and the specification amended. This laborious procedure resulted in the Women's Reserve Section undertaking the writing and approval of all specifications for Women's Reserve clothing.

Uniform Regulations
The original draft of the present uniform regulations, MCWR, published in August 1943, was formulated in the Reserve Division and approved by the Uniform Board, the Commandant of the Marine Corps and the Secretary of the Navy. Uniform regulations were distributed to all posts and stations to which women were attached and to each Women's Reserve Officer. Subsequently, numerous changes and additions were made as a result of Board recommendations and suggestions from posts and stations. The Uniform Regulations for Marine Corps Women's Reserve, approved by the Secretary of the Navy on 30 April 1945, supersede all regulations previously and contain General Regulations, Special Regulations, Tables of Uniforms, List of Illustrations and Index.

Federal Standard Stock Catalog
The Federal Standard Stock Catalog, WR Clothing, was published and distributed in order to familiarise posts and stations with all items available for Marine Corps Women's Reserve personnel. This document lists all Women's Reserve items in alphanumerical sequence, giving the stock number and size. It also lists items of men's clothing available for issue to women reservists.

Uniform, Service/Dress, Winter, WR

The uniform, service, winter, WR, consisted of a jacket, usually worn with winter service skirt, although the jacket could be worn with the slacks, covert, WR, when prescribed. The uniform jacket was of forest green material, tailored, with notched lapels, four slash pockets, sleeves finished with traditional 'Marine cuffs', and fastened by three dull-bronze standard Marine buttons. The jacket also had shoulder straps, each fastened by a small bronze Marine button. Officers or Enlisted bronze Eagle, Globe and Anchor (EGA) emblems were worn on the lapels.

Officers and Enlisted wore the same style jacket, with either Officer-quality or Enlisted-quality buttons (see Appendix 3). NCO rank insignia was forest green on scarlet background, the same as the male Enlisted Marine NCOs.

The skirt when worn was a six-panel, standard 'A' cut with a two-inch waistband and side zipper and single-button fastening. The hem of the skirt was to extend one and a half inches below the knee.

Left: Winter service uniform

Left and right: Winter service uniform, Enlisted. Note PFC stripes and FMF-Pacific shoulder patch

Slacks, Covert, WR, when worn with the jacket, were of forest green material with a pleated waist and two-inch waistband, zipper and single-button fastening on the left side. The slacks had a single internal hanging pocket on the right side.

The winter jacket was worn by both Officers and Enlisted with a khaki blouse (shirt), long-sleeved with two breast pockets closed with a top pointed flap, fastened by a single bone button. The shirt had no shoulder straps; Officers wore rank insignia in miniature on the collar. A scarf, service, khaki, WR (necktie) was worn with the blouse. Also for Officers, an alternative white blouse (shirt) was authorised for winter dress uniform. Worn with a forest green service scarf (necktie), tied four-in-hand, the shirt was long-sleeved with two breast pockets, same as the khaki shirt. Miniature rank insignia was worn on the shirt, in the same way as on the khaki service shirt. NCO rank insignia was forest green on khaki, same as male NCO insignia.

Headwear was the cap, service, winter, WR, for both Officers and Enlisted (see headwear, page 95). Seamed beige hose (stockings) were worn with Cordovan brown shoes, either Oxfords or bow-fronted pumps. When conditions allowed, e.g. if working indoors, the jacket could be omitted, and the wearing of a khaki blouse and scarf with either the winter uniform skirt or covert slacks could be prescribed.

Left: Slacks, covert

Right: Officers' winter dress white shirt and scarf

THE UNIFORMS

Forest Green 'Vandergrift' Jacket

With the Marine Corps Uniform Boards showing interest in the Army's 'Ike Jacket', designs were produced for what became the forest green 'Vandergrift' jacket. Some male Marines had had their forest green four-pocket jacket tailored into a short jacket on the design of the Australian Battle Jacket, issued to Marines after Guadalcanal whilst in Australia and New Zealand.

Some WRs had followed their male counter-parts by having one of their forest green service coats cut down and tailored into an 'Ike' jacket. Although unofficial, this practice resulted in the Battle Jacket, WR, being reviewed by the WR Uniform Board in 1945, but with the end of WWII and the disbandment of the Marine Corps Women's Reserve, the jacket was never put into production.

Surviving examples of cut-down WR service coats exist, the jacket being worn with either the forest green skirt or the forest green covert slacks.

Right: WR forest green 'Ike' jacket

Right: WR forest green 'Ike' jacket

THE UNIFORMS

Uniform, Service, Summer, WR

The uniform, service, summer, was a two-piece uniform consisting of a jacket and skirt made in green-and-white-striped material, originally Plisse Crepe but soon replaced by Seersucker.

The jacket was of a tailored fit, short sleeved with an open neck and four patch pockets, each with a pointed top flap fastened by a single button. The jacket fastened with five buttons.

The jacket had shoulder straps of the same material, each fastened by a single button. Buttons for the jacket were originally of white bone or composite but changed in late 1944 to green composite with the standard Marine eagle/anchor facing.

It was soon apparent that Officers rank worn on the shoulder straps was difficult to see, so Officers were authorised to wear shoulder boards of spruce green material, fastened by the shoulder strap button and by the rank insignia at the shoulder.

Left: Summer service (late)

Left: Summer service (early)

Right: Summer service with green composite buttons (45 Regs)

The uniform skirt was of a standard 'A' line, six-panel design, in the same green-and-white-stripe material, with a two-inch waistband and a button and zipper fastening on the left side. The button was a single white, bone or composite.

NCO rank insignia was of spruce green stripe, on a white background. Stripes were originally authorised to be worn singly on the left sleeve but were worn later on both sleeves.

Headwear for the summer service uniform was initially the Hat, Service, Summer, WR, but was replaced in 1944 by the Cap, Service, Summer, Garrison, WR (see headwear, page 93–94).

Collar insignia was dull-bronze EGAs (Enlisted or Officers) for the summer uniform. The purse, if carried, had a spruce green cover and shoulder strap (see accessories, page 101). Seamed beige hose (stockings), silk or rayon, or lisle whilst in ranks, were authorised wear, with brown Oxfords as per the winter uniform. White cotton gloves were optional wear with the summer uniforms.

Left: Summer service 'A' (43 Regs)

Left: Officers shoulder boards

THE UNIFORMS

Uniform, Summer Service B and C, WR

As an alternative to the summer dress uniform and for off-duty wear, the summer service green and white uniform could be worn with dress cap and collar emblems along with the summer dress cap (see headwear page 94). Footwear was to be white pumps (see accessories page 102). This was included in the 1943 Regulations under the title Summer Service B, but was subsequently changed in the 1945 Regulations, as was the specification for Summer Service C described below.

Summer Service C uniform for off-duty wear was the summer green and white uniform worn with the summer dress cap. Cap and collar emblems were to be dull bronze and footwear was to be brown pumps or Oxfords (see accessories page 102). There was no summer service C uniform prescribed for Officers in the 1943 regulations.

Right: Summer service 'B' (43 Regs)

Right: Summer service 'C' (43 Regs)

Uniform, Undress, Summer, LS

In 1945 there was an addition to the summer uniform wardrobe of a long-sleeve version of the summer service jacket.

The Coat, Service, Summer, LS, was made of the same green and white seersucker material worn with the summer service skirt. The jacket had long sleeves finished with 'Marine cuffs', was open-necked and fastened with three green composite Marine buttons. The jacket had four patch pockets, each with top flap closure fastened by a single green composite Marine button, as well as shoulder straps in the same material, fastened by a single green composite Marine button.

The summer uniform, LS, was worn with the summer dress cap, cap and collar emblems were dress (Enlisted or Officers), and footwear was either white or brown pumps. Purse was to have the summer green cover and white gloves were optional wear. Officers wore spruce green shoulder boards with their rank insignia as per the short-sleeved summer uniform.

Right: Summer undress (LS)

THE UNIFORMS

Uniform, Dress, Summer, WR

The summer dress uniform was an optional item for Enlisted WRs but mandatory to Officers. This uniform was the most striking and admired of all the WR uniforms.

Consisting of a jacket and skirt in white twill for Enlisted, and twill or Palm Beach for Officers, the jacket was modelled on the summer service uniform jacket, open necked and with short sleeves. Enlisted personnel also unofficially had their dress whites made of Officer-quality Palm Beach cloth. The jacket had four patch pockets, each closing with a top flap fastened initially by a single white button and later by a single gilt eagle/anchor button. The jacket had shoulder straps of the same material, again initially fastened by a single white button, later a single gilt eagle/anchor button. The jacket fastened down the front with five white bone buttons, later replaced by gilt eagle/anchor buttons.

The uniform skirt was the same six-panel 'A' line skirt in white cotton, with a two-inch waistband and zipper side fastening, as for the summer service uniform skirt. Collar emblems were the dress emblems, gilt for Enlisted and silver and gold for Officers. Officers wore the spruce green shoulder boards with rank insignia as for the summer service uniform.

The summer dress uniform was worn with beige hose and white pumps. Headwear was the summer dress cap with gilt side buttons and dress emblem (either Enlisted or Officers). Purse, if carried, was to have the spruce green cover and shoulder strap. Gloves were to be white cotton and were an optional wear item.

Right: Summer dress (Palm Beach)

Far right: Summer dress

Uniform, Dress, Summer, 'A', Officers, WR

Without question, the Officers' summer dress 'A' uniform was the most striking of all the WR uniforms, outshining any of the other services' female uniforms. The uniform consisted of jacket and skirt in white Palm Beach cloth. The skirt was a standard six-panel style, and the jacket was also of Palm Beach cloth of the same cut and style of the winter forest green service/dress coat. It was long sleeved, with 'Marine cuffs', four slash pockets and fastened by three gilt eagle/anchor buttons. The coat had shoulder straps with a single, gilt, small eagle/anchor button and was collarless, intended to be worn with an open-necked, short-sleeved white silk blouse.

The lack of a collar to the coat gave rise to the problem of where to place the Officers dress collar emblems. The answer was to have them placed on the shoulder straps, towards the shoulder seam with the rank insignia placed between the emblem and the gilt button. This led to great controversy with the male Marines, especially due to not knowing if the approaching Officer was a 2nd Lieutenant or a 2-star General with all the 'ironwork' on their shoulders.

The Summer Dress 'A' uniform was worn with the Summer Dress/Service hat with gilt side buttons and Officers dress cap emblem. Handbag, if carried, had the spruce green cover. Shoes were the white dress pumps and the wearing of white gloves was optional. Hose was to be beige rayon or nylon, seamed.

Right: Officer summer dress 'A'

THE UNIFORMS

Utility/Work Wear, WR

In the beginning it was not envisaged that women Marines would be involved with many 'dirty' jobs, but employed mainly in clerical or office related jobs. The WR wardrobe did, however, have work wear available to the individual WR but was not a mandatory requirement. Work or utility wear initially consisted of Coat, Utility, WR and Overall, Utility, WR.

Coat, Utility, WR

Made of lightweight sage green cotton and modelled on the men's three-pocket HBT Utility Coat, it had three patch pockets, two lower and one top left, the same as on the man's, with the black EGA/USMC pocket stencil. The coat fastened by four composite buttons unlike the man's, which fastened by US Marine Corps tack buttons. Cuffs were button adjustable, again by two composite buttons.

Right: Work wear

Overall, Utility, WR

Again made from sage green cotton, the overalls were of the 'bib and braces' type with a bib front, fastened by buttoned shoulder straps, each with two composite buttons. The overalls had two rear open-top patch pockets and fastened initially at the back by four composite buttons. This was later changed to a four-button side fastening on the left side. The overalls were worn either with a white 'skivvy shirt' or the shirt, utility, WR, under the utility coat.

Headwear was usually the cap, utility, WR. This was a 'Daisy Mae' hat made from the same sage green cotton. It had a six-panel crown with a stitch-reinforced brim and was usually worn with the brim turned up all round.

Below: Bib and braces – late pattern

Above: Bib and braces – early. Note cap, utility

THE UNIFORMS

Shirt, Utility, WR

Again made of sage green cotton, the utility shirt was short sleeved and front fastening with no pockets. This shirt was worn with either the overalls, utility, WR, or with the slacks, utility, WR.

Right: Shirt, utility

Slacks, Utility, WR

These were of sage green HBT material with side button fastening and two rear patch pockets, each with a pointed top flap secured by a single composite button. The cuffs had tab and button adjusters, fastened by composite buttons.

Left and right: HBT utility slacks

THE UNIFORMS

Coat, Utility, WR (revised)

The sage green utility coat was found to be too lightweight for some of the heavier work such as maintenance and mechanical work. Initially WRs involved in these heavier jobs were issued men's HBT coats and trousers. These were eventually replaced with the WR HBT slacks and the coat, utility, WR (revised). The coat was basically the three-pocket utility coat made from sage green HBT material, as the slacks, complete with black EGA/USMC pocket stencil on the left breast pocket.

Footwear for work/utility wear was either low quarter Oxfords (no heel) or men's issue field shoes (Boondockers). Later, WRs could purchase WR field shoes but these were scarce and highly prized. They were usually kept highly polished and worn with the forest green covert slacks (see footwear page 103).

Headwear for the utility slacks and coat was usually the cap, garrison, utility, WR.

Right: HBT jacket, utility

Culotte, Utility, WR

Intended to be summer-issue workwear, the utility culottes were made of the same sage green cotton, split-skirt, reaching to 1.5 inches below the knee (same as the other uniform skirts). The culottes fastened on the left side with zipper and single composite button. It was intended to be worn with the Shirt, Utility, WR and Hat, Utility, WR. Footwear was usually low quarter Oxfords (see footwear page 103).

Above and left: Culottes, utility

Suit, Exercise, WR

Physical fitness has always been high on the agenda for a US Marine; it was also so for the WRs. Initially, for daily exercise the WRs wore a two-piece dress and shorts of green-and-white striped seersucker, the same material as for the summer service uniform. The dress was short sleeved with a single open topped breast pocket on the left. The hem of the dress was to be 2 inches below the knee (same as for all skirts). The dress fastened down the front, full length, by 10 white bone buttons (same as the buttons on the summer service uniform) and had a waist belt, with no buckle, of the same green and white seersucker material.

The shorts were worn under the dress, having elasticated cuffs (for modesty), the cuffs reaching just above the knee. The shorts had a half elasticated waistband and fastened on the left with two white bone buttons. Due to the similarity of the exercise suit to the summer service uniform the colour and design of the suit was soon changed to the brown and white striped seersucker 'peanut suit.

Above: Green and white exercise suit

Left: Peanut suit – early (no skirt)

Suit, Exercise, WR – Peanut Suit

The WR exercise suit or 'peanut suit' as it was commonly referred to (due to its light brown colour and crinkled appearance), consisted of a one-piece shorts and blouse in brown-and-white striped seersucker material, buttoned down the front with six composite buttons. The suit had drawstring cuffs on the shorts (for modesty) and was short-sleeved. Later production suits had a removable skirt, made from the same material as the suit and buttoned down the front with seven composite buttons. It was intended that the skirt be worn whilst moving from barracks to the exercise area.

Brown or white exercise/sports pumps were usually worn with white ankle socks to accompany both of the exercise suits, sometimes low quarter Oxfords could be worn when the exercise suit was worn for duties other than exercise i.e. cleaning barracks etc.

Right: Peanut suit – later (with skirt)

Below: Peanut suit cleaning brigade

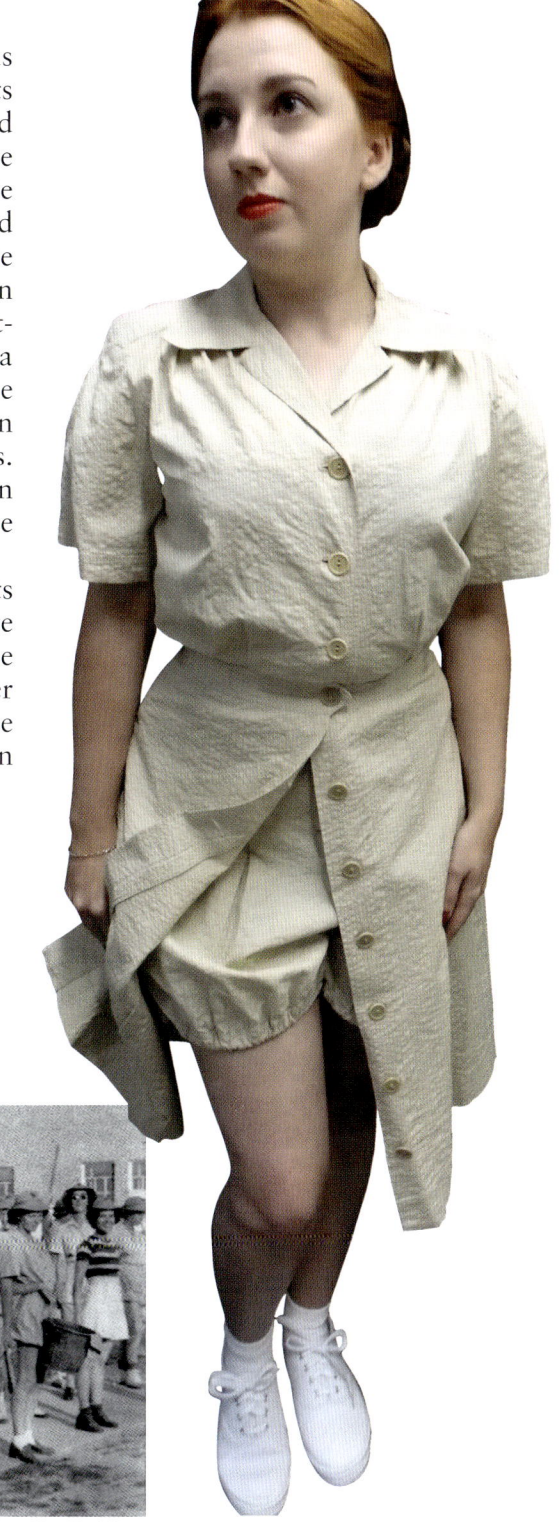

THE UNIFORMS

Vest, Alpaca Pile Lined, WR

Intended to be worn with the Uniform, Utility, WR, the alpaca-lined vest was of sage green cotton with brown alpaca-pile lining. It was a sleeveless vest (waistcoat) fastening with a full-length zip.

Left and right:
Vest, alpaca

Red Cross Knitted Tank Top

Not an issue item as such, many WRs were gifted these knitted tank tops by local Red Cross volunteers.

Right: Red Cross tank top

Coat, Trench, WR, c/w Liner and Hood

The trench coat was of double-breasted design fastened with three pairs of composite buttons (all buttons were composite brown plastic) with a storm collar fastened by a single button. It had a belted waist, the belt fastening with a green composite open-faced buckle. The coat had hip slash pockets with button closures and through access. Cuffs were adjustable, each fastened by a single button, as were the shoulder straps. The coat had a single 20-inch rear central vent fastened midway by a single button.

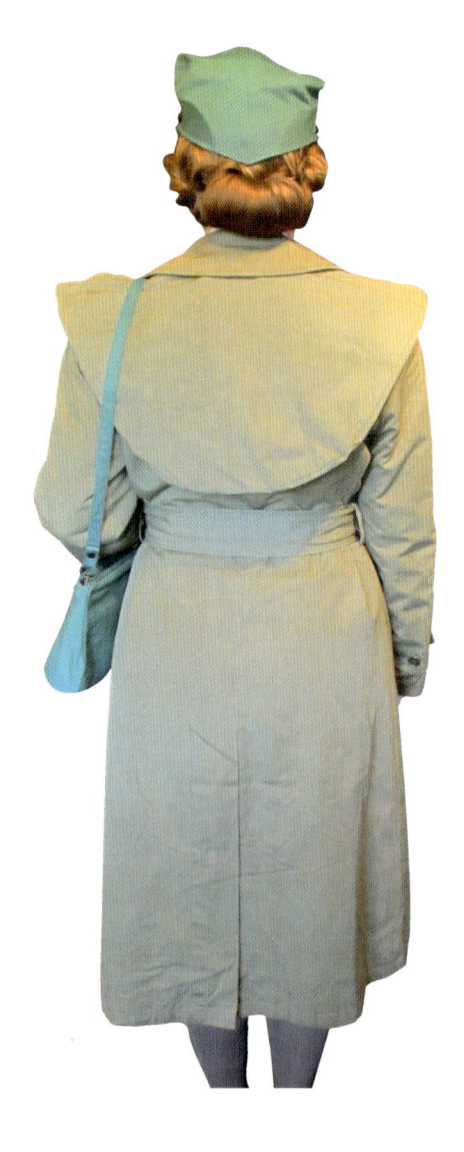

Above: Field coat, WR (front)   **Above:** Field coat, WR (rear view with hood)

The trench coat had a button-in blanket liner, also a removable cowl-type hood, which allowed the winter or summer kepi to be worn. The trench coat was issued to both Officers and Enlisted and worn with Cordovan brown leather gloves and either the red wool muffler with winter dress or the white rayon muffler for summer dress. No rank insignia was worn on the trench coat.

Below: Field coat hood

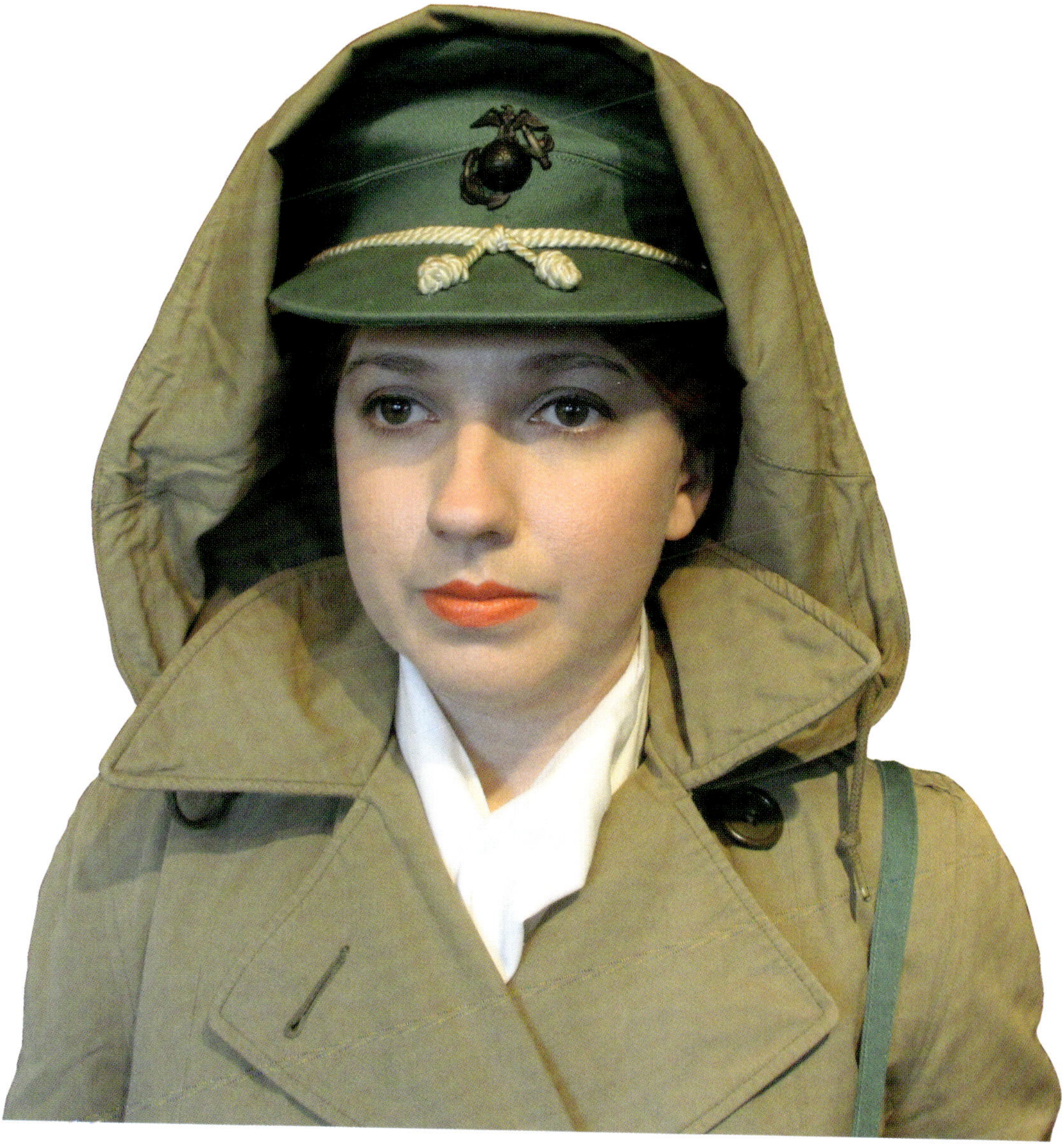

Raincoat, Lightweight, WR

An optional item available to both Officers and Enlisted personnel. The lightweight raincoat was of sage green treated rayon, cut on the same lines as the WR overcoat. It was double-breasted, fastened by three pairs of composite brown plastic buttons. The raincoat had slash pockets left and right, fastened with a single composite button. It also had shoulder straps fastened by a single composite button and a storm collar with notched lapels fastened with a single composite button.

The back of the raincoat, as with the overcoat, was pleated left and right of a central 16-inch vent fastened midway by a single composite button, and finished with a half belt, fastened by two composite buttons.

Rank insignia was not authorised to be worn on the lightweight raincoat.

Above: Lightweight rain coat

Overcoat, Officers, WR, and Overcoat, WR

Originally only part of the Officers wardrobe but was later available to both Officers and Enlisted.

The overcoat was of forest green woollen material, the same as for male Marines (Officers could be tailor made) and sateen lined. The overcoat was double-breasted, fastened by three pairs of bronze Marine buttons. It had a storm collar with notched lapels, fastening with a single bronze Marine button. The coat had Marine cuffs with internally hung pockets with top flaps. The back of the overcoat was pleated left and right of a central 18-inch vent with a half belt fastened by two dull-bronze Marine buttons. The coat had shoulder straps, each fastened by a single small bronze Marine button.

Rank insignia was authorised to be worn; Officers insignia on the shoulder straps, NCO rank stripes were the winter forest green on red.

The overcoat was usually worn with the winter service dress with red wool muffler and Cordovan leather gloves.

Above: Overcoat, officers/enlisted

Jacket, field, WR

The field jacket was identical to the man's version, with the exception of the front button closure being reversed for the female version. The jacket was of khaki cotton with slash pockets, shoulder straps, and tab and button cuff-adjusters, also having tab and button adjustment to the jacket hips. The jacket had a sewn-in blanket liner and was fastened down the front with a zipper and button closure. (All buttons were composite brown plastic.)

Rank insignia was authorised to be worn: Officers rank on the shoulder straps; NCO rank stripes were forest green on khaki as per the service shirt.

The field jacket could be worn on post in lieu of the winter service jacket with the skirt or covert slacks with shirt and scarf, also with the utility slacks or culottes as exercise wear.

Above: Field jacket – note Aviation Squadron patch

Left: Field jacket

HEADWEAR

Hat, Summer Service WR

The first headwear for the summer service uniform was a round-brimmed 'Daisy Mae' made of spruce green cotton twill. Originally made with a snap brim, fashioned after the WAVES and SPARS snap brim hat; the WAVES and SPARS hat had two crowns, one navy blue and one white, which snapped into the navy blue brim. Either the white- or navy blue-crowned hat was worn as per uniform of the day.

The crown of the WR summer service hat was of the same colour as the brim and buttoned in place with six small white buttons, rather than snapped in place like the WAVES and SPARS hat. It was soon apparent that the removable crown of the summer service hat was superfluous, being of the same colour material as the brim, and so specification was changed to have the crown sewn into the brim.

The summer service hat was usually worn with the brim turned up at the rear and down at the front. A grommet hole at the front allowed for fixing the bronze service cap-size Eagle, Globe and Anchor emblem, which was the same size as the man's service cap emblem. The summer service hat continued as part of the summer service dress until it was replaced in late 1944 by the newly authorised summer garrison cap.

Above: Summer service hat – early button brim

Right: Summer service hat – late stitched brim

Cap, Garrison, Summer, WR

Made of spruce green cotton twill with white piping, the summer garrison cap was part of the uniform changes authorised by the WR Uniform Board in late 1944, in conjunction with the approval for WRs to serve overseas (primarily at Marine establishments on the Hawaiian Islands).

The summer garrison cap had a grommet hole on the front left side for the fixing of the collar size; the left side EGA was in dull bronze (Officers wore miniature rank on the right side). The cap was worn as specified in the new 1945 WR Uniform Regulations.

Cap, Dress, Summer, WR

The summer service/dress cap was of spruce green cotton twill, modelled on the same lines as the winter service/dress cap. The summer cap had a white cap cord rather than the scarlet cap cord on the winter cap.

Worn with dull-bronze side buttons and with bronze, cap-size Eagle, Globe and Anchor front and centre when specified for summer service uniform, and worn with gilt side-buttons and gilt, cap size, EGA for summer dress uniform (for Officers, silver and gold EGA was worn with Officers summer dress uniform).

The summer service/dress cap was specified headwear, with the summer service uniform, either short sleeve or long sleeve and the summer dress white uniform and Officers summer dress 'A' uniform.

Right: Cap, dress, summer

Below: Cap, garrison, summer

Cap, Service/Dress, Winter, WR

Headwear for winter service/dress uniforms for both Officers and Enlisted women was the cap, service, winter. Made from the same forest green material as the winter uniform, the cap was of kepi style with a standing front and a sweeping crown, finishing at the back to a point reminiscent of the Marine pointed cuff. The peak of the cap was covered with the same forest green material, but had no leather chinstrap like the male service cap; instead it had a decorative 'Montezuma red' cord across the peak, held in place by a small dull-bronze button either side. The cord finished in a double knot front and centre with end tassels on the peak (stitched in place). The bronze cap-size EGA emblem – Officers or Enlisted – was worn on the cap front and centre.

Above: Cap, service/dress, winter

Cover, Rain, Cap, WR

A translucent rain cover, made of vinalyte-coated rayon voile, pale khaki in appearance, worn over either the winter or summer dress kepis. The cover incorporated a Havelock in the same material, covering the back of the head and fastened under the chin with a single hook and eye. The rain cover could be worn with either the field coat or the lightweight raincoat.

Left and right: Rain cover, cap

Cap, Garrison, Utility, WR

Adopted in March 1944 for wear with the utility uniform and slacks, utility, WR, the garrison cap was of sage green HBT material, modelled on the lines of the cap, garrison, summer, WR. The garrison cap had a grommet hole on the front left side for fixing the coat and collar-size bronze EGA emblem. Officers wore small size rank insignia on the right side of the cap.

Right: Cap, garrison, utility

Officers service cap and collar emblems

Enlisted service cap and collar emblems

Officers dress cap and collar emblems

Enlisted dress cap and collar emblems

HEADWEAR 97

Above: Poster for Elizabeth Arden Montezuma Red

U.S. MARINE CORPS: WOMEN'S RESERVE

ACCESSORIES

Accessories for the various uniforms were kept to a minimum and where possible were of popular design.

Scarf, Service, Khaki, WR, and Scarf, Dress, Officers, WR
The winter service dress for Officers and Enlisted personnel prescribed a khaki scarf (necktie) tied 4-in-hand, to be worn with the khaki shirt waist. (Pre-tied versions were also available to purchase.)

For the Officers winter dress uniform, the khaki shirt was replaced with a white shirt and the khaki scarf was placed with a forest green scarf, again tied 4-in-hand.

Above: Scarf, khaki and forest green

Gloves, Cotton, Brown or White, WR, and Gloves, Leather, Lined, Enlisted Man's

Gloves were authorised wear for both winter and summer service/dress uniforms. Dark brown cotton or Cordovan brown leather for winter uniforms, white cotton were authorised for the various summer service/dress uniforms.

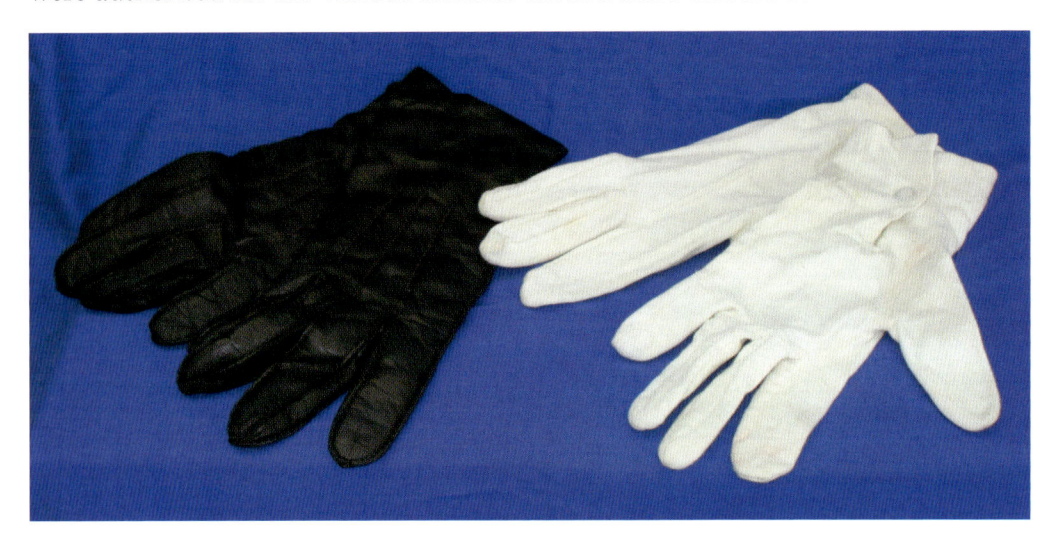

Above: Gloves, brown service and white dress

Handbag, Leather With Strap, WR, and Cover, Cloth, Green With Strap, WR

Permitted when not in ranks, the WRs had a leather handbag, Cordovan brown, made of buffalo hide with matching leather shoulder strap (always carried on the left shoulder, over or under the uniform shoulder strap, thus leaving the right arm to render a salute.) The handbag had a khaki lining with divided pockets and a separate coin purse.

For use with the various summer service and dress uniforms, the handbag had a spruce green cotton cover with matching shoulder strap that replaced the Cordovan leather strap.

Right: Handbag c/w summer cover, coin purse and mirror

Above: Handbag

Below: Handbag, summer cover

ACCESSORIES

Muffler, Rayon, White and Wool, Red, WR

Authorised to be worn with the winter service dress field coat, field jacket and overcoat was the muffler, wool, red, WR. For wear with the summer service uniform, with field coat or raincoat over, the muffler, rayon, white, WR, was authorised.

Right: Red and white mufflers

Shoes/Footwear

WRs were required to purchase their own footwear initially: Cordovan brown Oxfords, with or without moccasin toe, and with a maximum 2.5-inch heel. In 1944, dress pumps in Cordovan brown and white were authorised for wear with the summer dress/undress uniforms.

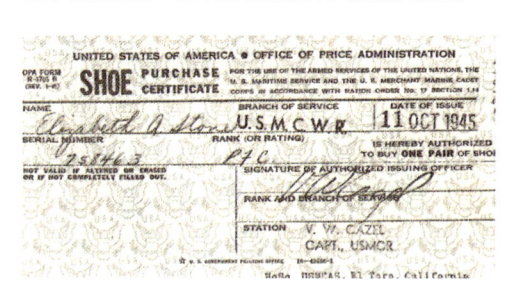

Above: Shoe purchase certificate

Above: Service Oxfords

Above: Dress white pumps

Above: Service brown pumps

Work footwear was either low quarter Oxfords in Cordovan brown or, initially, men's field shoes (Boondockers). Eventually the WRs were issued with their own field shoes in russet brown. One much coveted item of footwear were the Aviation Brogues, usually worn with the forest green slacks and usually by WRs attached to Air Stations. All WRs were required to purchase rubber galoshes for wear over their Oxfords and low quarter Oxfords in inclement weather.

Above: Low quarter Oxfords

Above: Men's field shoes (Boondockers)

Above: Field shoes

Right: Aviation brogues

Right: High quarter galoshes

Above: Low quarter galoshes

ACCESSORIES

Hose

Stockings were to be worn with all summer or winter uniforms. For Enlisted, lisle cotton hose was authorised, and Officers could wear rayon- or nylon-seamed hose. Enlisted could also wear rayon- or nylon-seamed hose when working indoors or off duty. The cotton lisle hose was loathed by WR's Officers and Enlisted due to the fact they were forever falling down and having to be constantly pulled up!

All stockings were worn either with garter belts, girdles or garters.

Right: Lisle cotton hose

Below right: Rayon hose

Below: 'We all hated Lisle stockings' (courtesy of Theresa Karas Yianilos)

782 Gear Issue to WRs

Although not generally issued to WRs, a limited 782 gear was issued to those selected for service overseas, in particular the Hawaiian Islands. Those WRs selected received additional training in the field, including the use of gas masks, erecting and striking shelter halves and transferring from ship to landing craft via cargo nets. (It must be remembered that there was still a threat from Japanese submarines during the voyage from mainland USA to the Hawaiian Islands.)

Above: 782 gear

ACCESSORIES

Above and below: 782 gear (front and back)

782 gear (so called after the record of issue on form NAVMC782–QM) issued to WRs consisted of pistol belt, first-aid dressing and pouch, canteen, canteen cup and cover, Officer M1936 haversack (Musette bag), mess can and knife, fork and spoon, shelter half complete with pole, pins and guy line, two blankets. Weapons, helmets and gas masks were not issued to WRs.

Upon arrival in the Hawaiian Islands the WRs turned in their 782 gear to the Quartermaster.

Left: WRs underwent gas-mask training like their male counterparts

Below: 782 gear

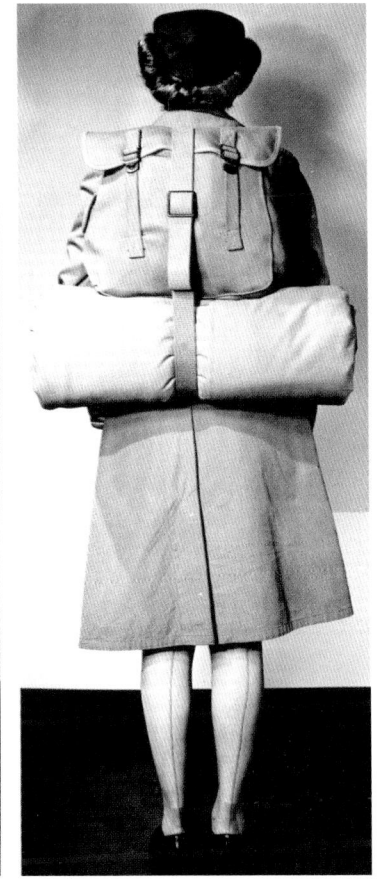

ACCESSORIES 107

U.S.
U.S.

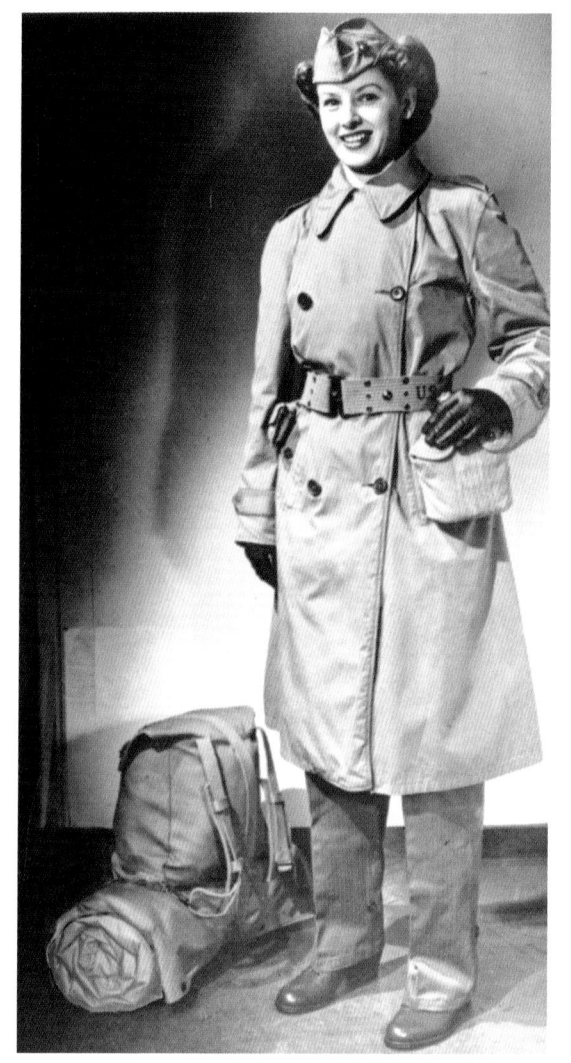

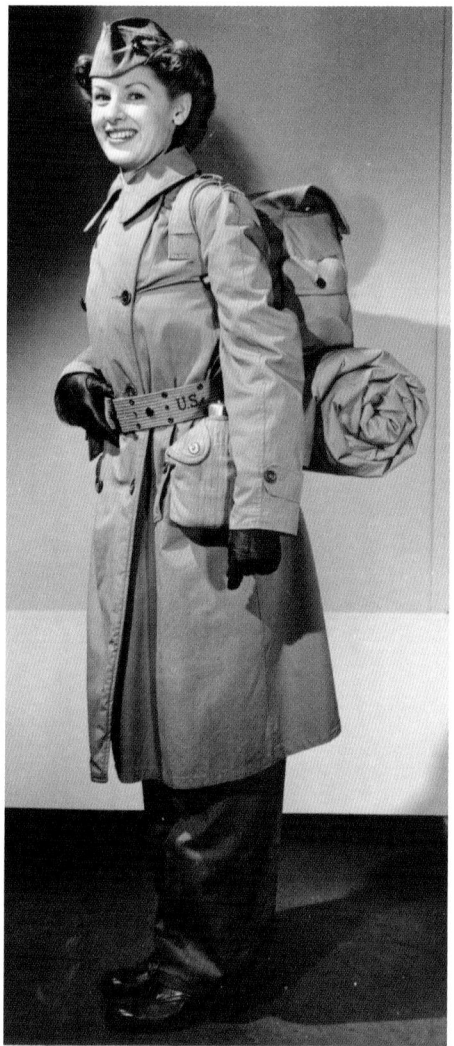

Above: 782 gear

APPENDIX 1
Quartermaster Photographs

The Quartermaster study of WR uniforms was undertaken after World War II and the disbandment of the Women's Reserve. All images are courtesy of the USMC Historical Section, MCRD, Quantico, VA.

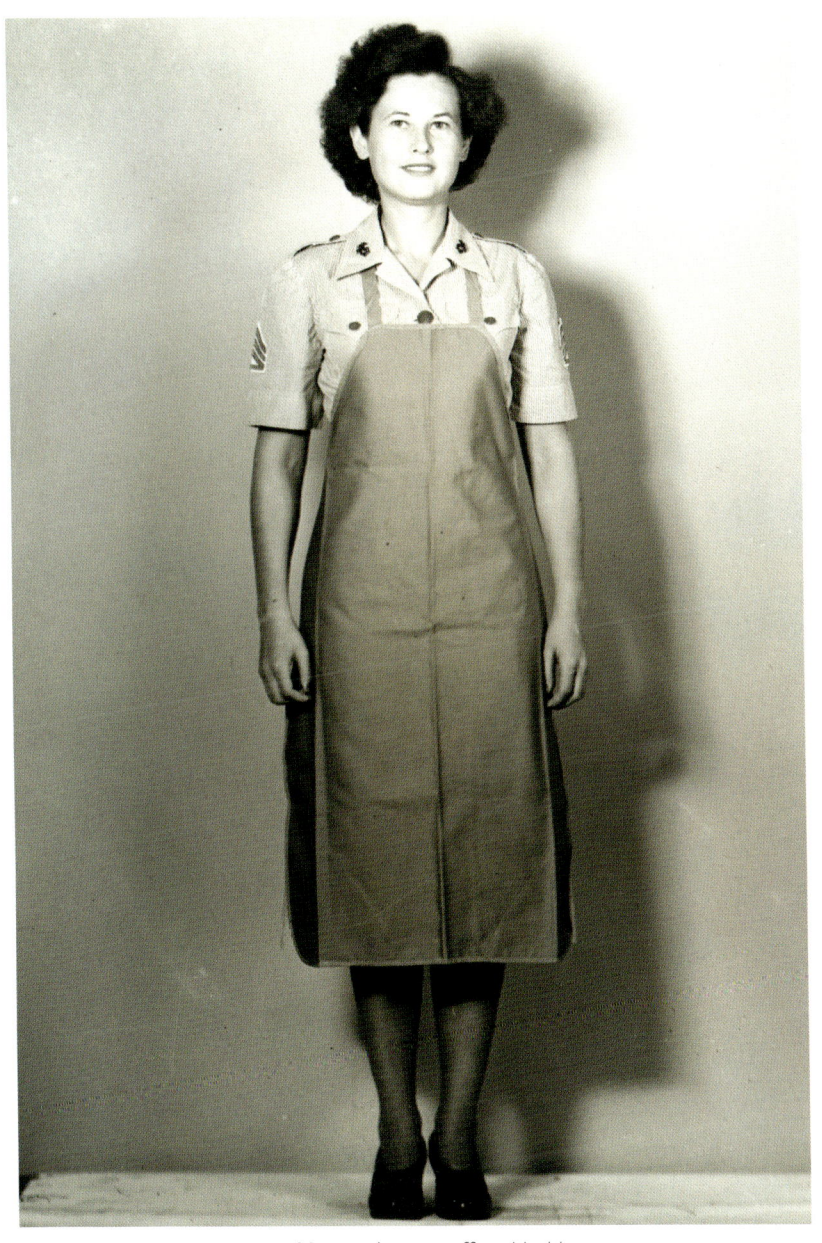

Above: Apron, office, khaki

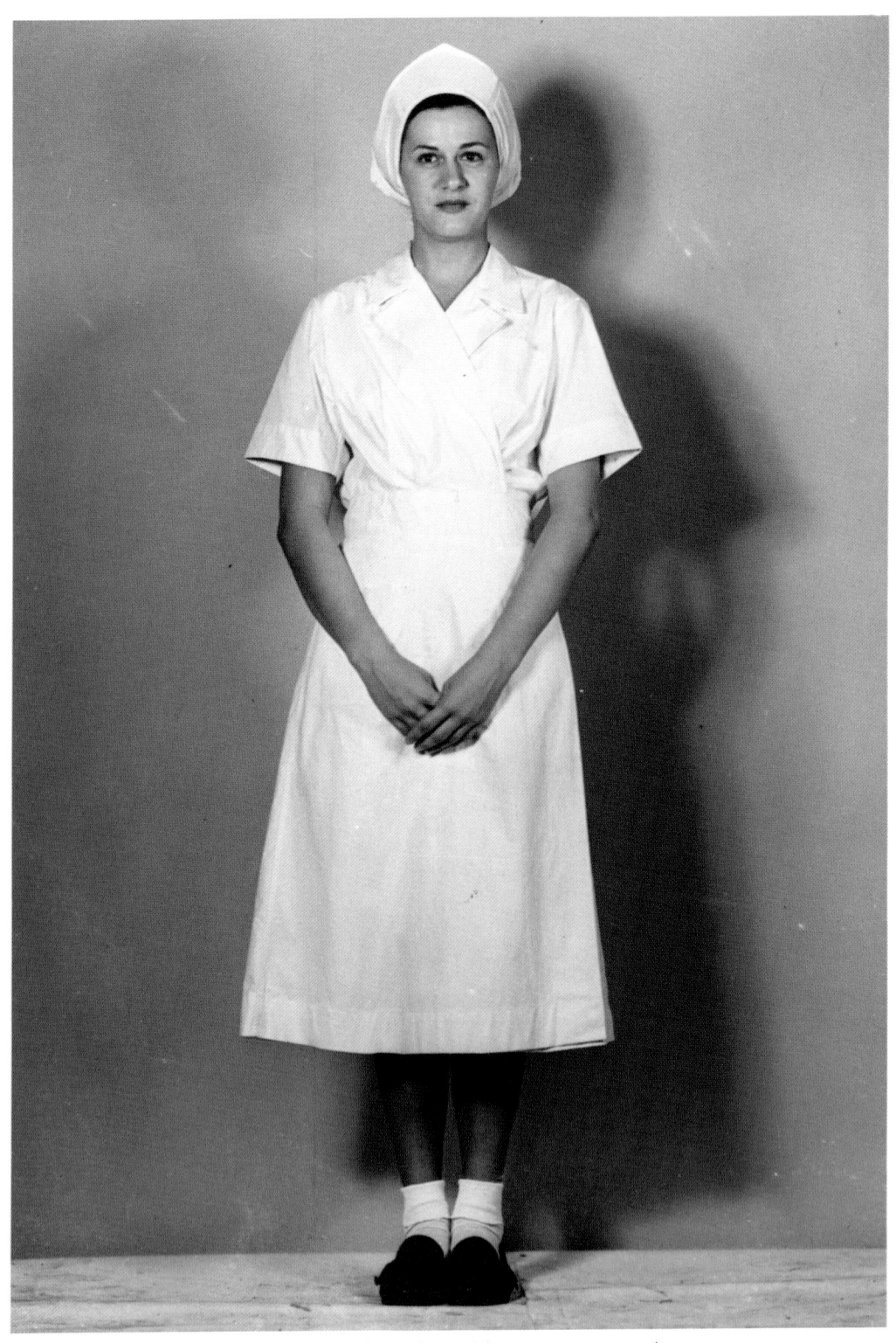

Above: Apron, bungalow, with cap, messwomen's

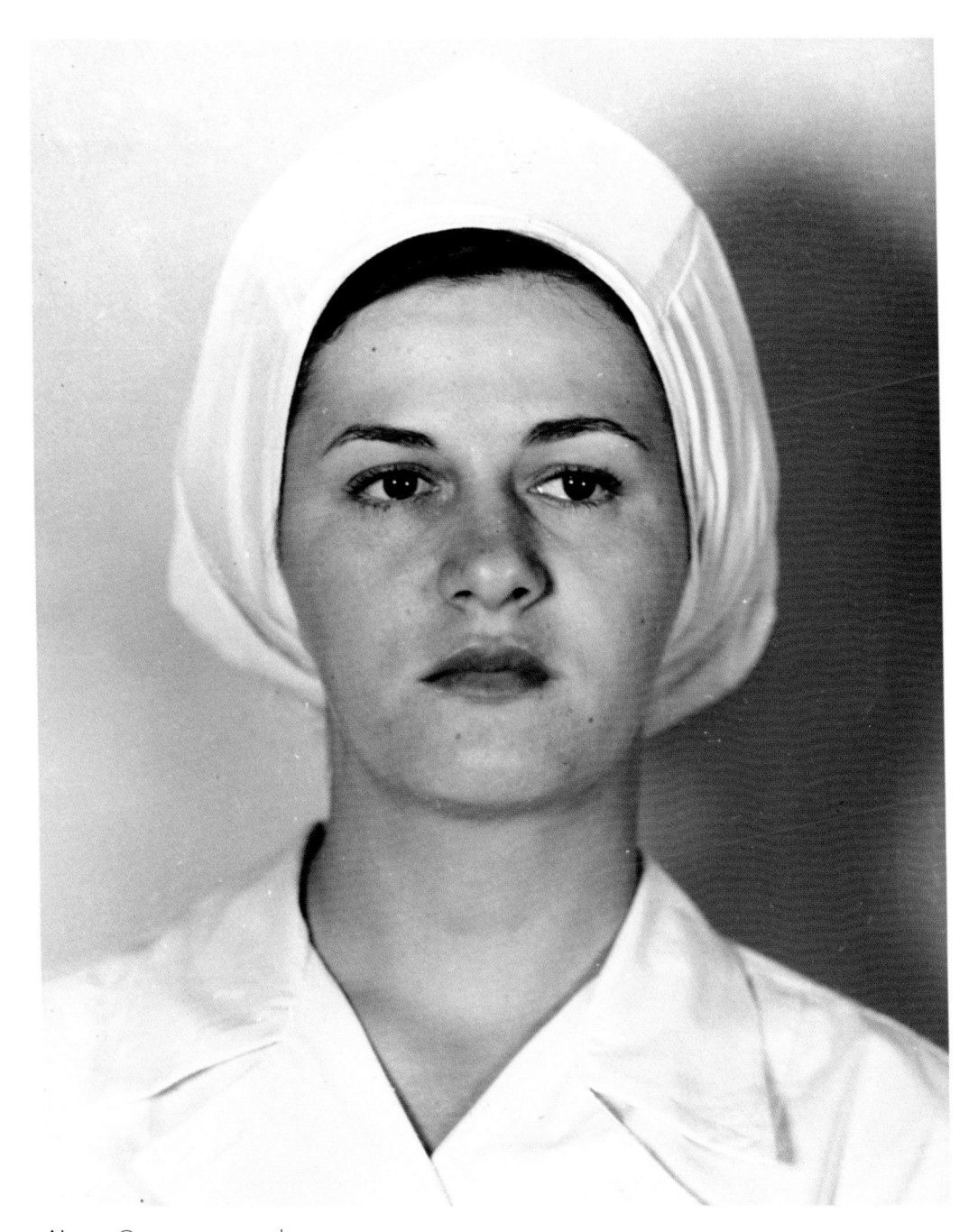

Above: Cap, messwomen's

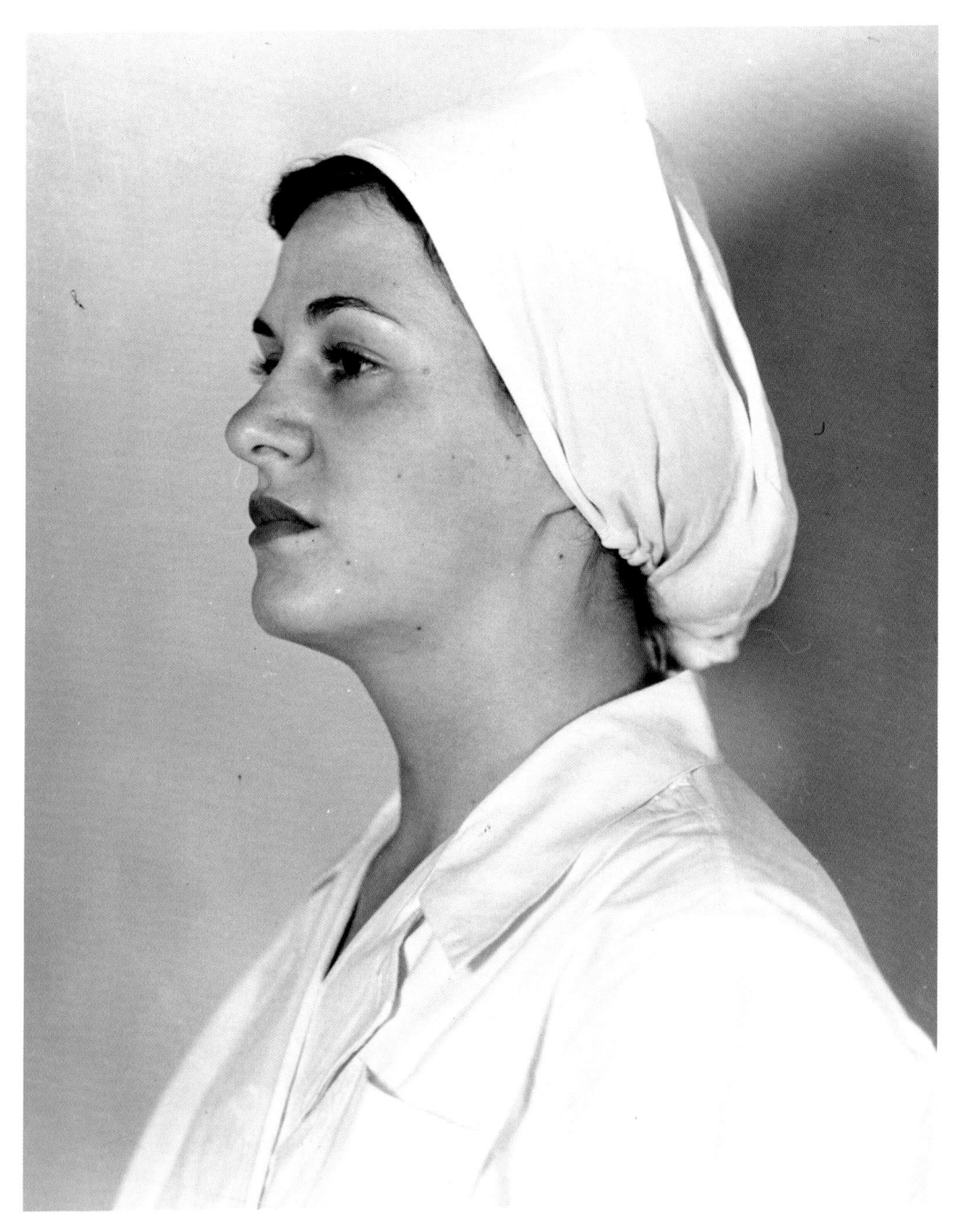

Above: Cap, messwomen's

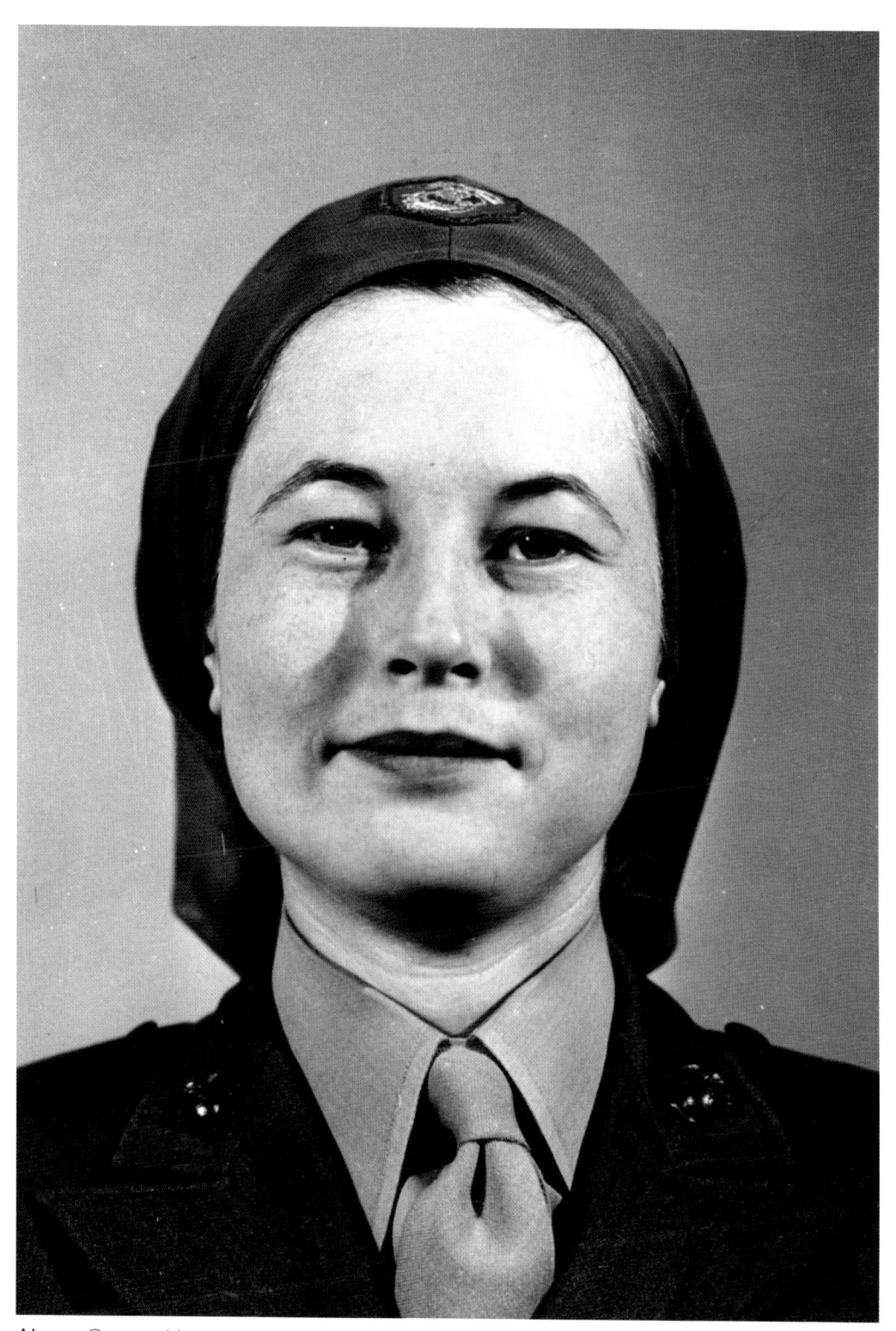

Above: Cap, machine operator

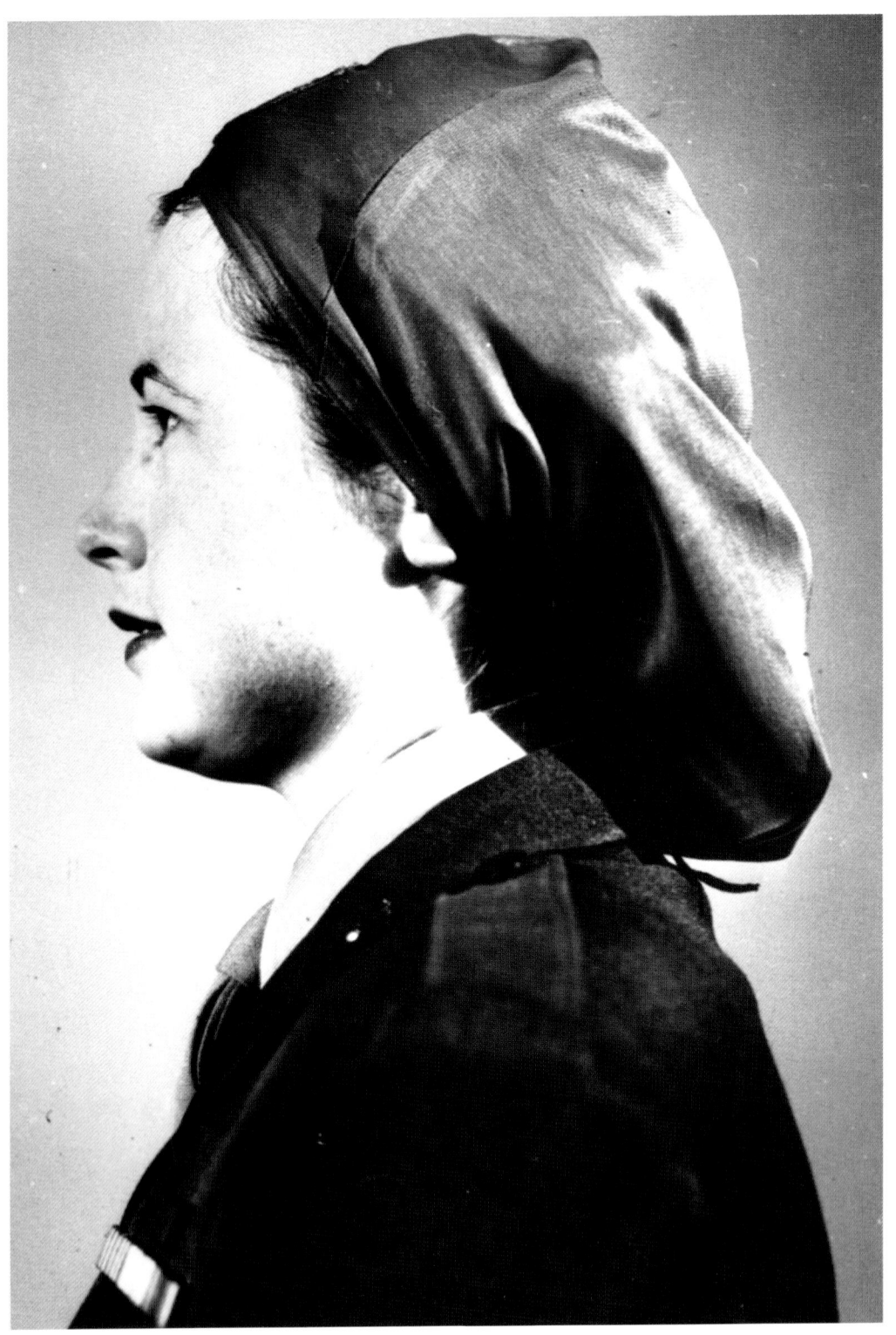

Above: Cap, machine operator

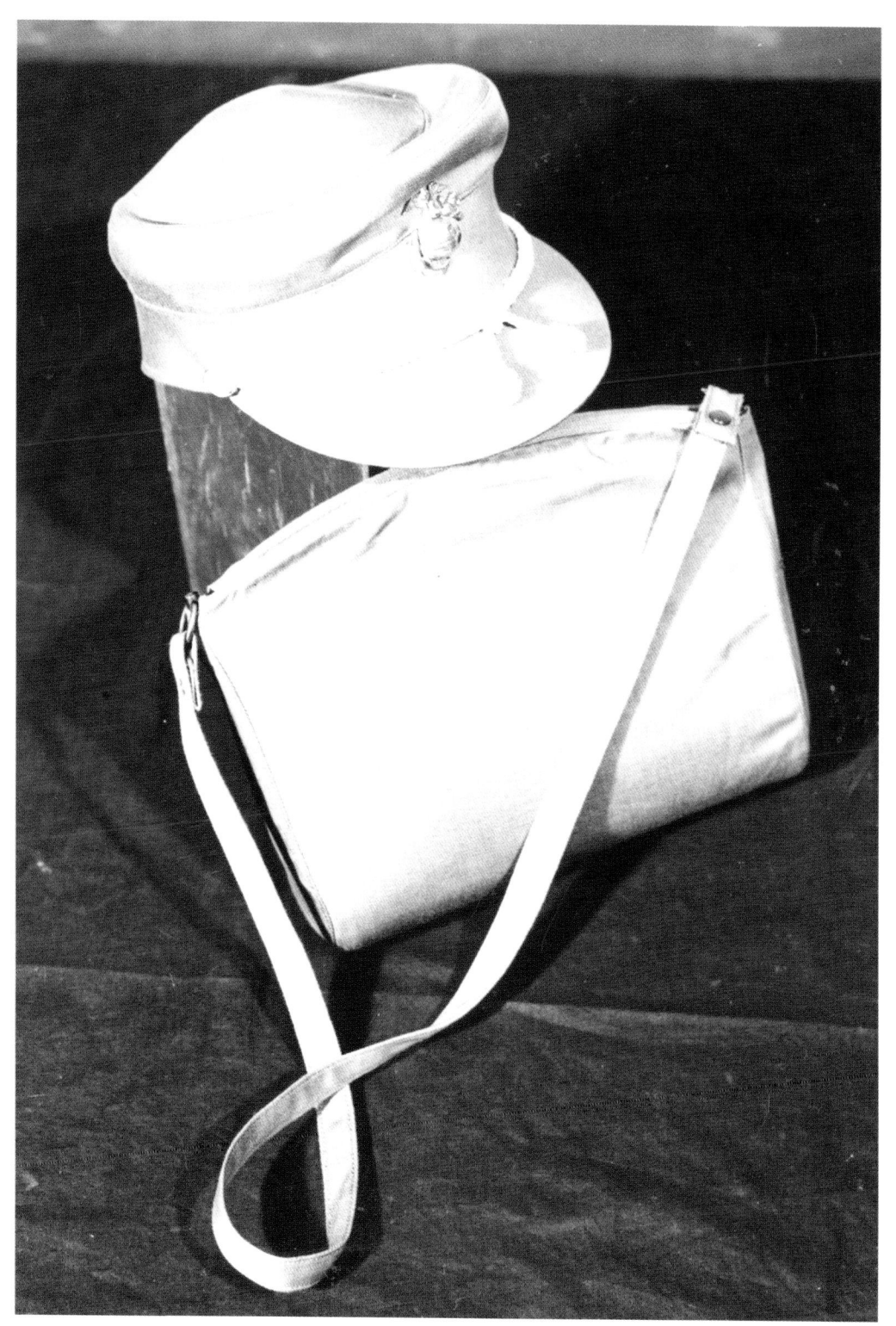

Above: Cap, spruce green, with handbag cover, spruce green

Above: Cap, winter service

Above: Cap, summer, dress, WR

Left: Cap, garrison, summer

Right: Cap, utility, with shirt, utility

All photos: Coat, trench c/w hood and liner

QUARTERMASTER PHOTOGRAPHS 119

Left: Coat, trench, liner

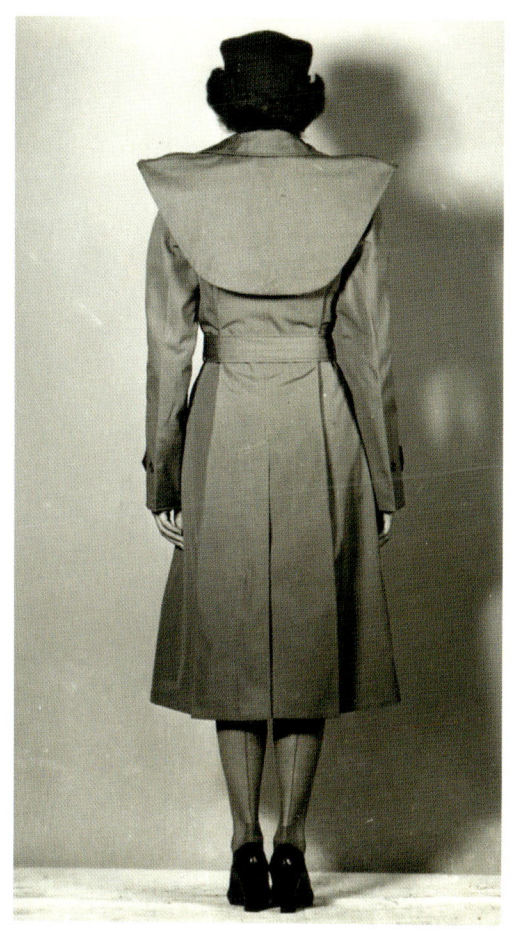

All photos: Coat, trench c/w hood and liner

QUARTERMASTER PHOTOGRAPHS

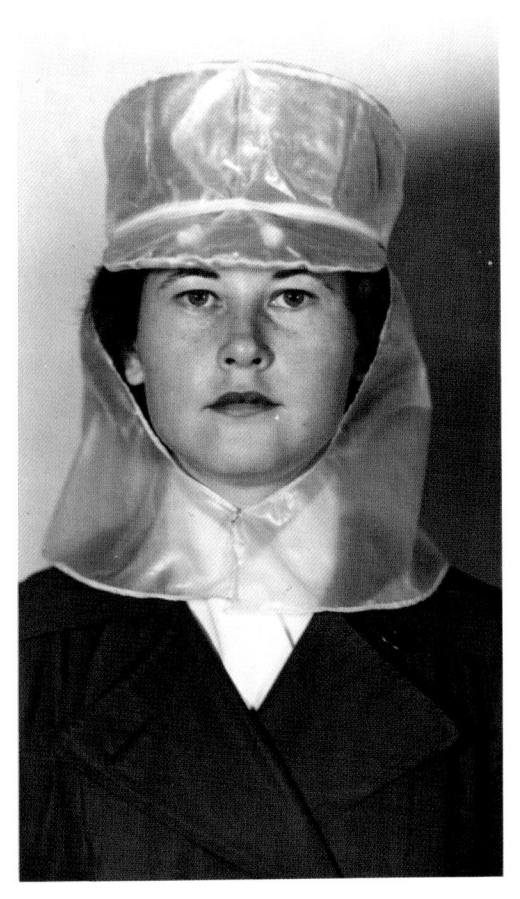

All photos: Cover, plastic, raincap

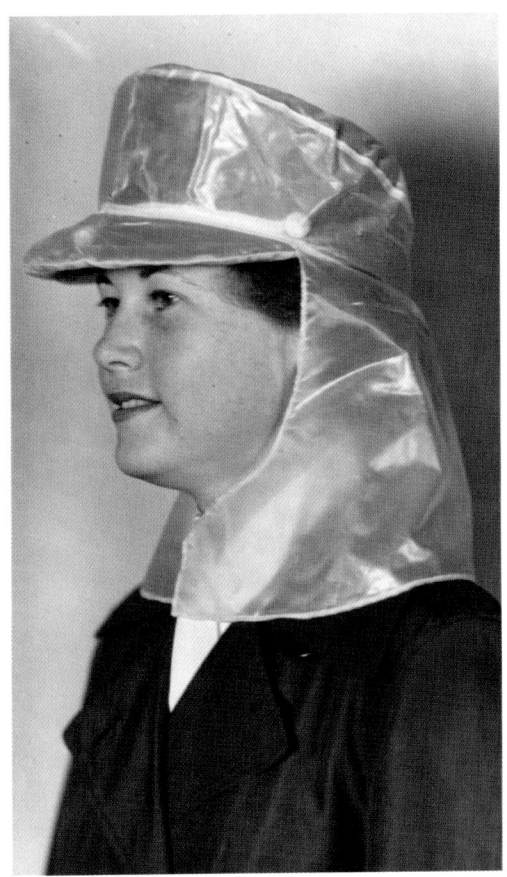

Above: Culotte, with utility shirt

Above: Culotte, utility

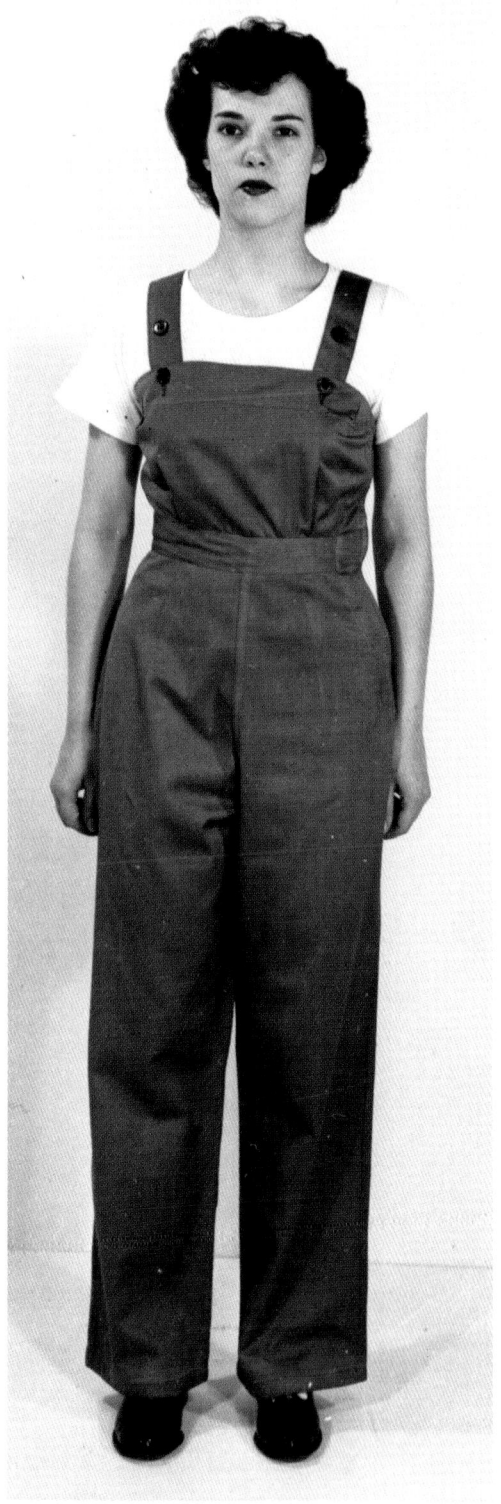

Above: Overalls, utility

Left and right: Overcoat, forest green kersey

QUARTERMASTER PHOTOGRAPHS

Left and right: Raincoat, lightweight forest green, rayon and cotton

128   U.S. MARINE CORPS: WOMEN'S RESERVE

QUARTERMASTER PHOTOGRAPHS 129

Above and right: Shirt, cotton, khaki c/w scarf (necktie), khaki

QUARTERMASTER PHOTOGRAPHS

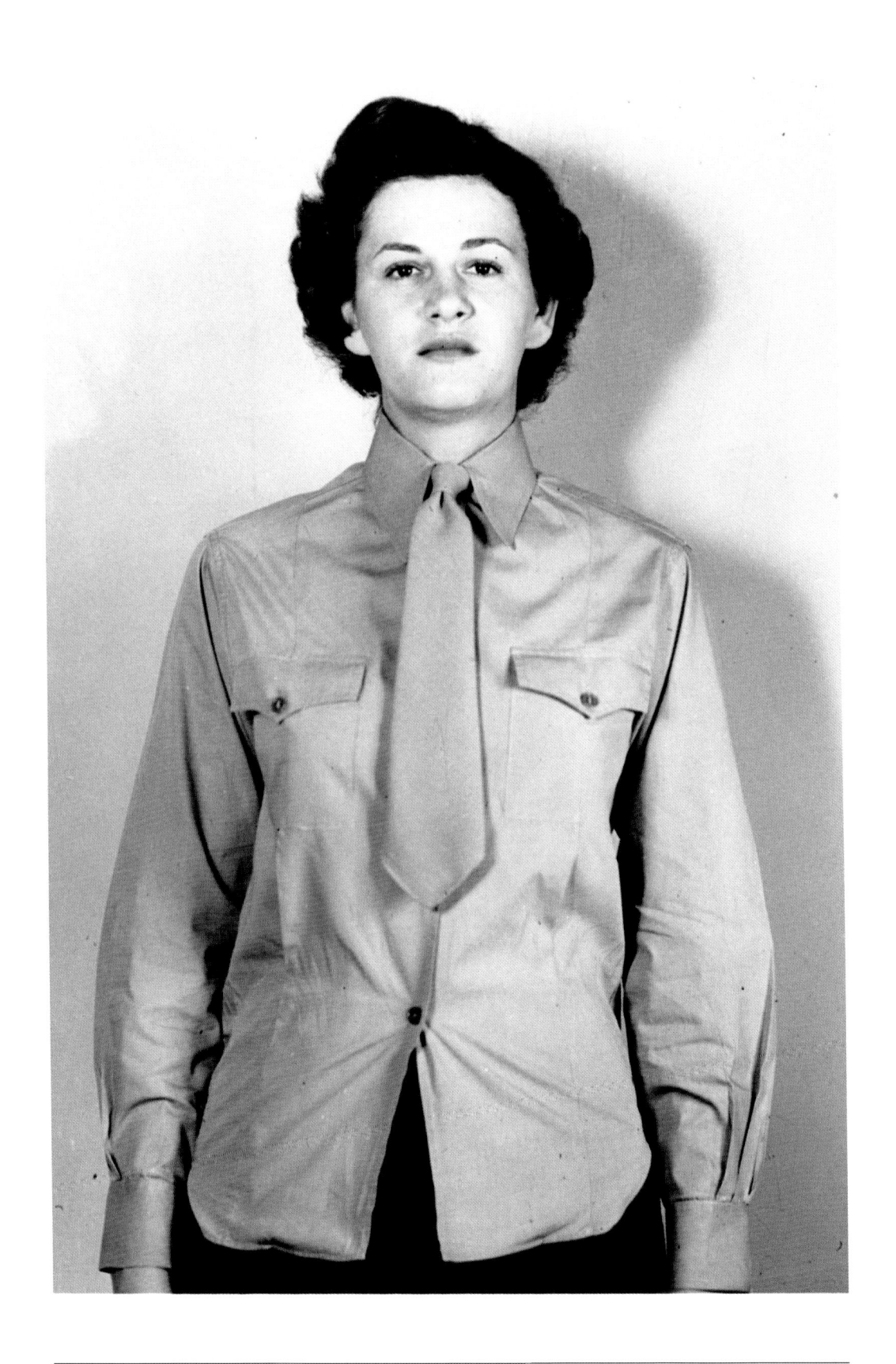

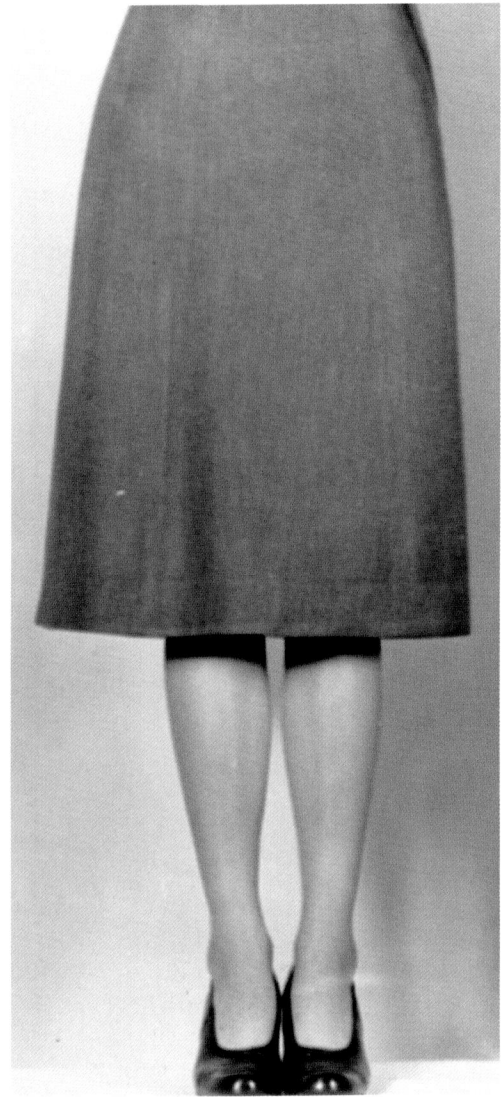

Above: Skirt, winter service

Left: Slacks, wool covert

Right and far right: Slacks, utility

QUARTERMASTER PHOTOGRAPHS

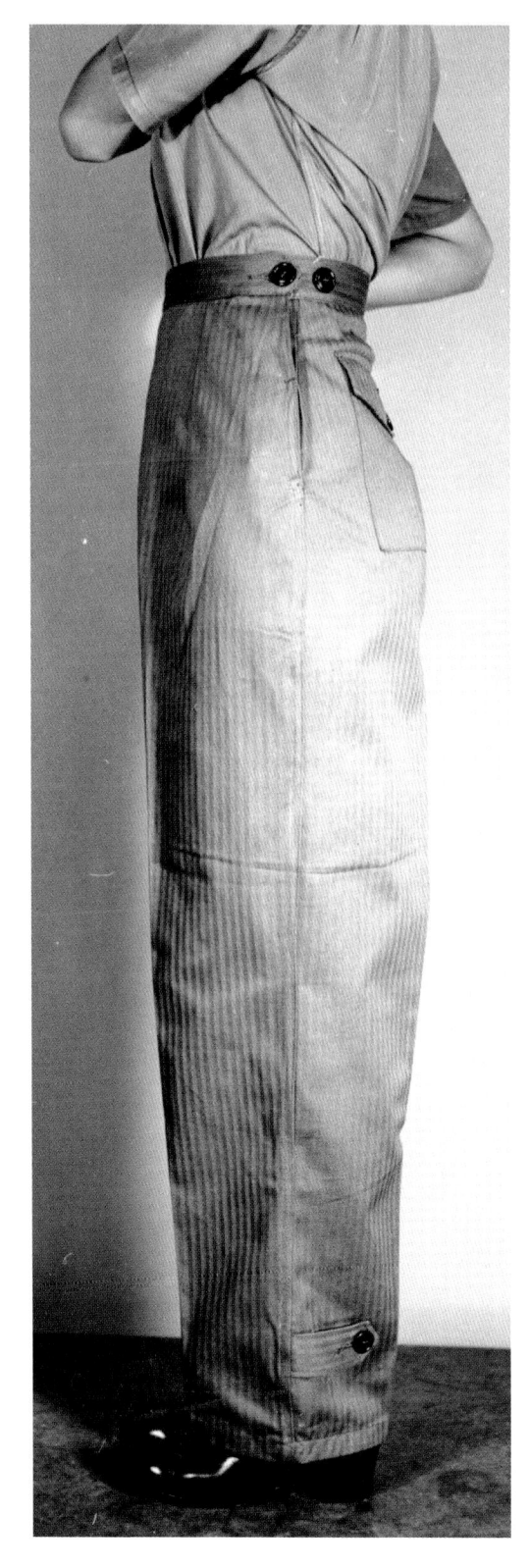

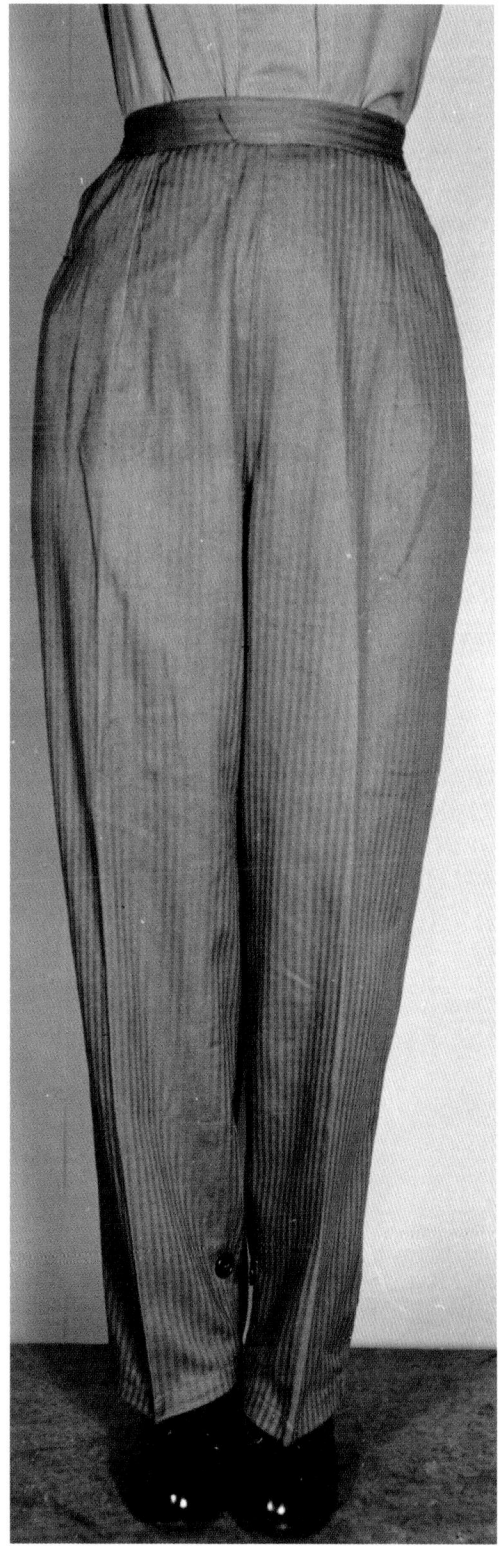

Above and right: Uniform, enlisted, winter service

QUARTERMASTER PHOTOGRAPHS

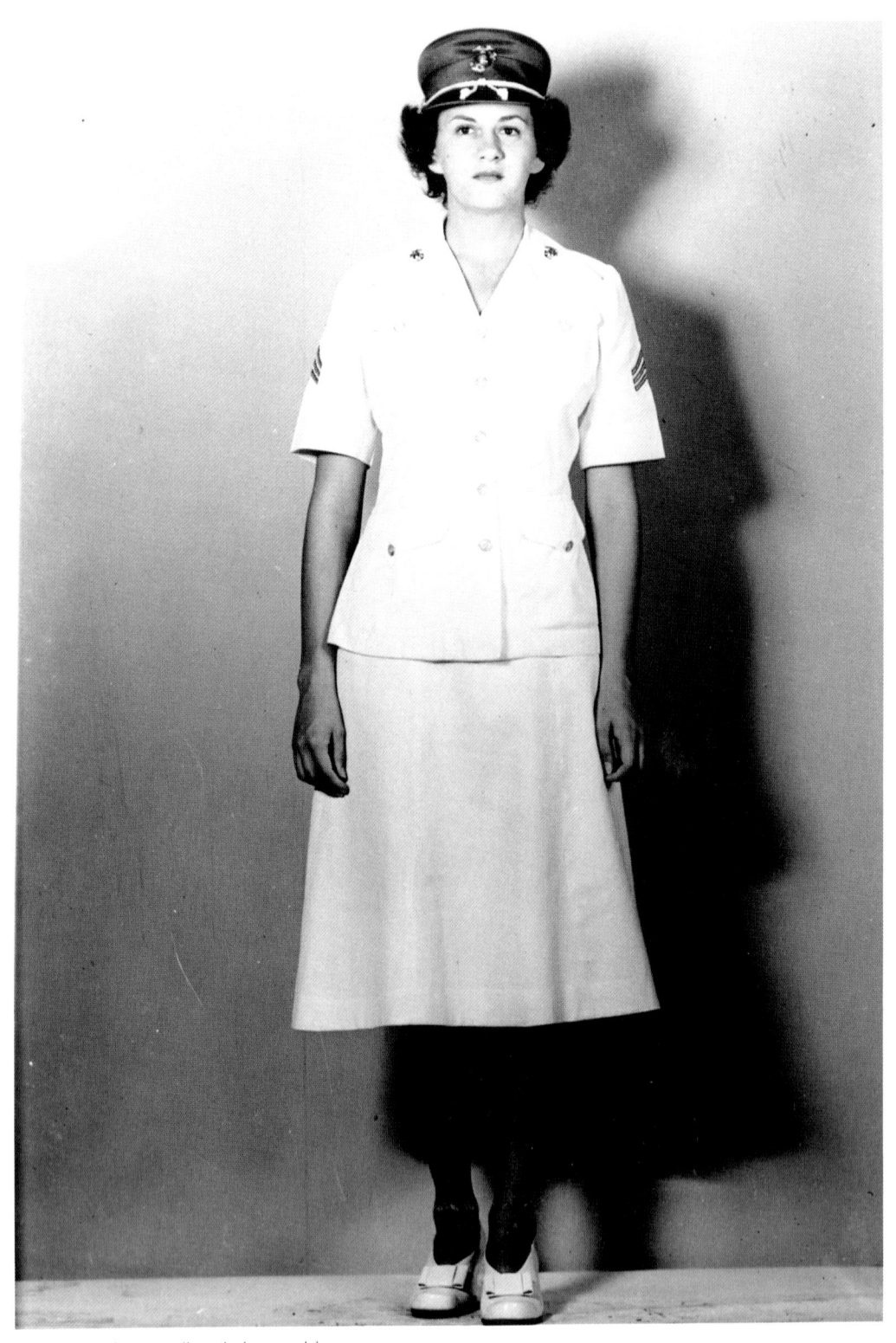

Above: Uniform, enlisted, dress white

Above: Uniform, undress, summer, LS

Above: Uniform, officer, summer dress 'A'

Above: Captain Anne A. Lentz – Uniform, officer, winter service

Above: Uniform, utility

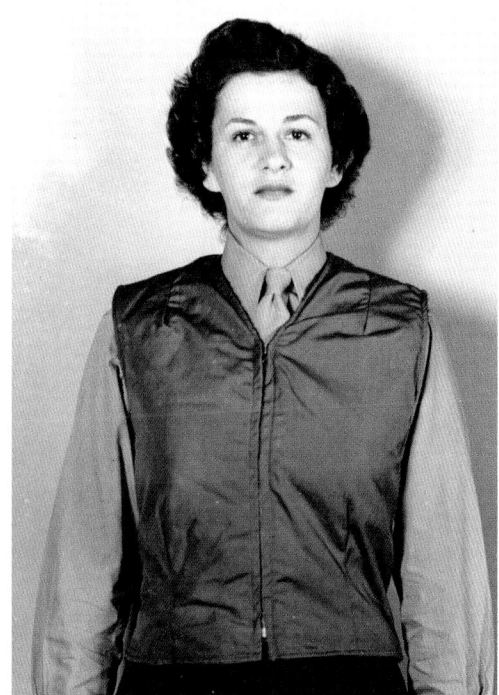

Above: Vest, alpaca pile-lined

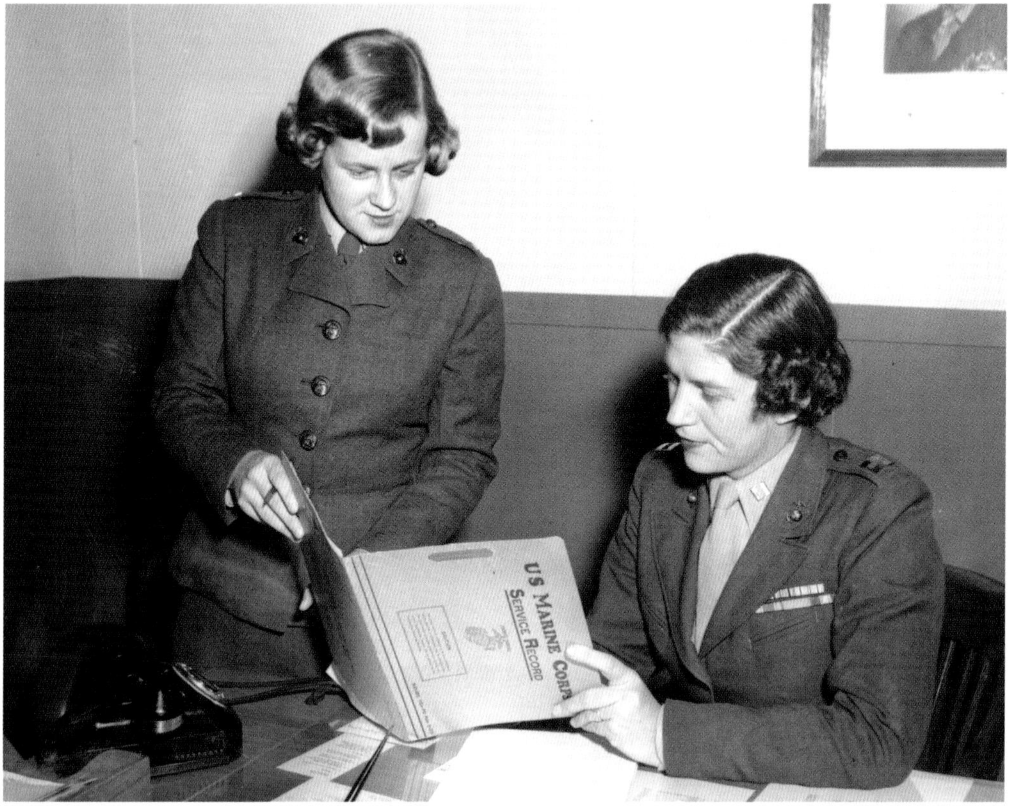
US MARINE CORPS
SERVICE RECORD

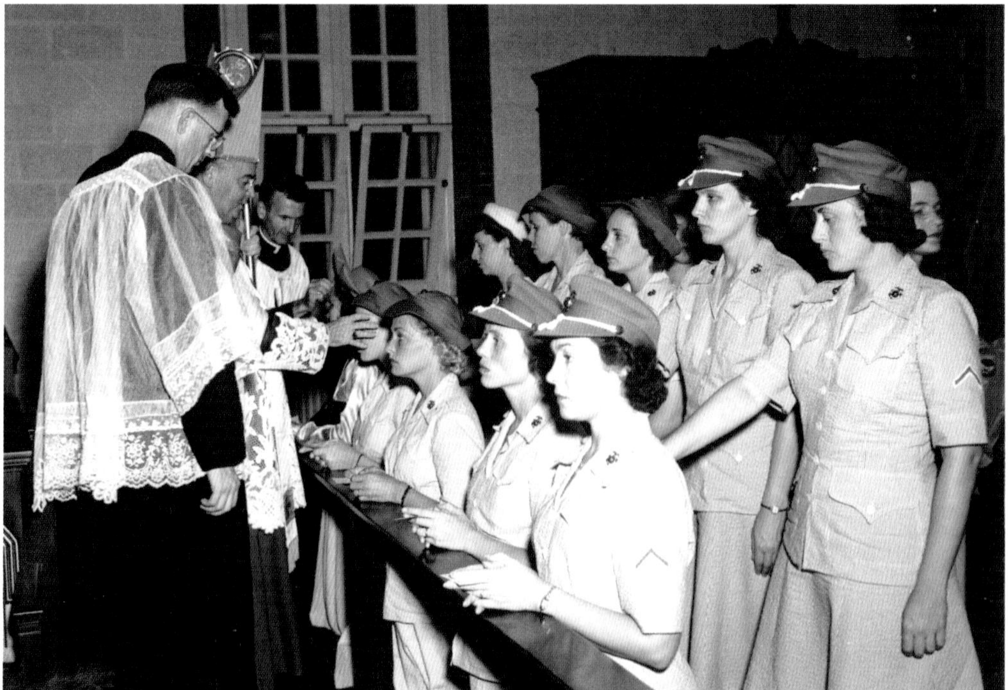

Above: Note early 'button brim' summer service hats

Opposite top: Note tailor-made jacket at left

Opposite bottom: WRs attend communion services

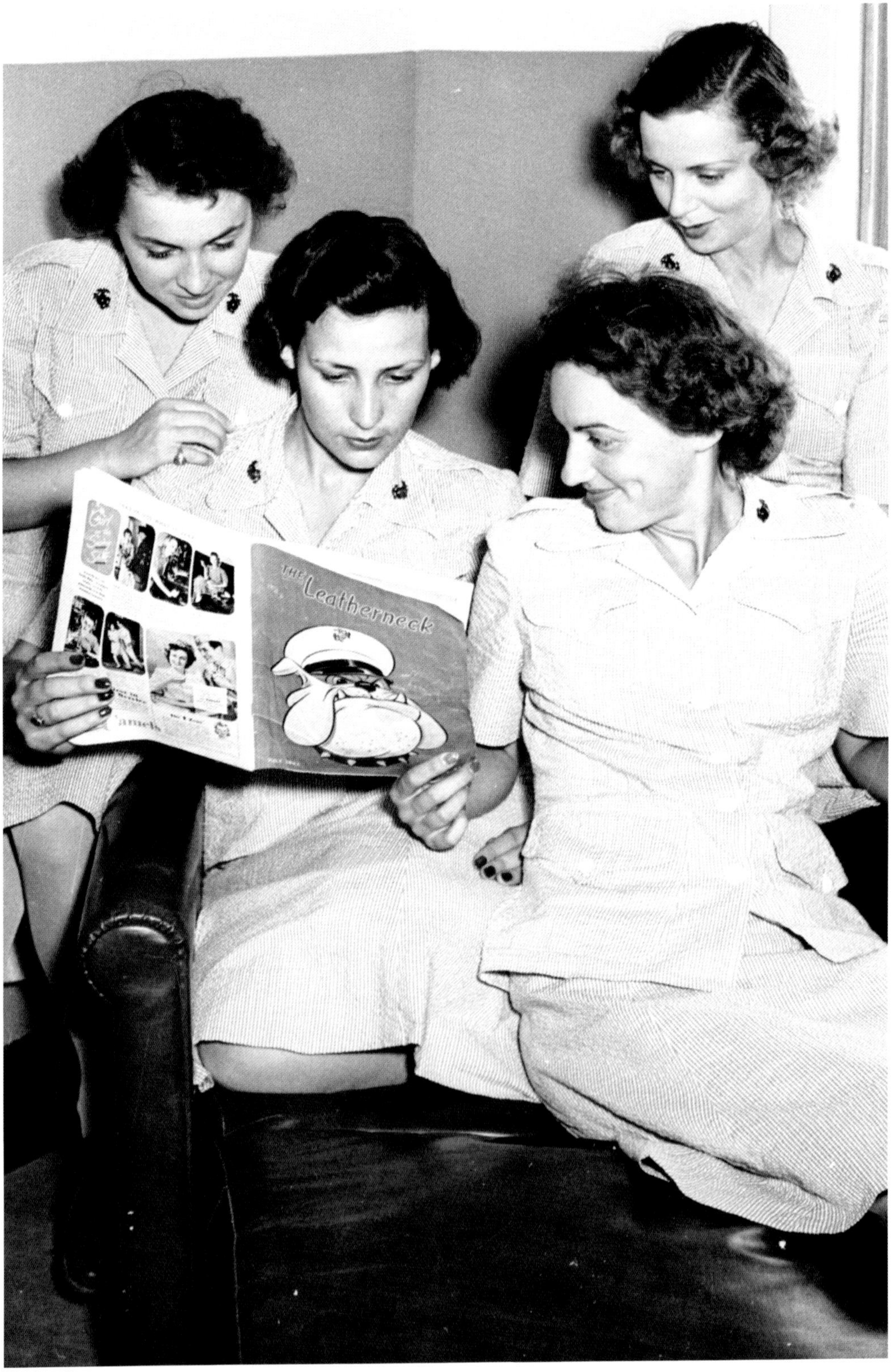
THE Leatherneck

Above: Summer service dress. Note mixture of early button-brim and, later, stitched-brim hats

Opposite: WRs appeared in several issues of *Leatherneck* magazine

Above: Cap, summer, garrison

Above and below: Women's Reserve receiving their colours

QUARTERMASTER PHOTOGRAPHS

Above and below: Women's Reserve retiring their colours

Above: Ruth Cheney Streeter – The first director of the United States Marine Corps Women's Reserve

APPENDIX 2
Jobs in which Women Marines Were Assigned During World War II

Accountant
Addressing or Embossing
 Machine Operator
Administrative NCO
Armorer, Aircraft
Artist
Auditor
Automobile Serviceman
Automotive Carburetor & Ignition
 Mechanic
Automotive Equipment Operator
Automotive Mechanic
Aviation Salvage Crew Mechanic
Aviation Supply Man
Baker
Band Leader
Bandsman, Bass Drum
Bandsman, Clarinet
Bandsman, Cornet or Trumpet
Bandsman, Euphonium or Baritone
Bandsman, Flute or Piccolo
Bandsman, French Horn
Bandsman, Saxophone
Bandsman, Oboe
Bandsman, Snare Drum
Bandsman, Trombone
Bandsman, Tuba
Barracks NCO
Beauty Operator
Boiler Firemen
Bookkeeper
Bookkeeping Machine Operator
Carburetor Mechanic, Aircraft
 (Designated Type)
Carpenter, Aircraft
Carpenter, General
Cashier
Chaplain's Assistant
Chauffeur
Chemical Laboratory Technician

Chemical Warfare Specialist
Chief Clerk
Chief Ordnance Man, Light Air Fire
 Control
Classification Specialist
Clearance Desk Clerk
Clerk, Administrative
Clerk, General
Clerk Typist
Code Clerk
Combat Correspondent
Commissary Man
Communication Chief
Control Tower Operator
Cook
Court Reporter
Crane Operator
Dispatcher, Motor Vehicle
Draftsman, Electrical
Draftsman, General
Draftsman, Mechanical
Draftsman, Topographic
Drill Instructor
Drum Major
Education Specialist
Electrician, Aircraft
Electrician, General
Electric Motor Repairman
Electroplater
Engine Overhaul Mechanic,
 Aircraft (Designated Engine)
Engineer Stock Man
Fabric Worker, Aircraft
Field Artillery Fire Control Man
Field Lighting Truck Operator
Field Musician
File Clerk
Filter Operator, Water Supply
Financial Typist, Clerk
Finger Printer

Fire Control Instrument Technician
Fire Fighter
First Sergeant
Freight Transportation Clerk
Gas & Oil Man
Guard
Gyro Mechanic, Aircraft
Heavy Artillery Fire Control NCO
Heavy Machine Gunner
Heat-Treater
Hydraulic Mechanic, Aircraft (Designated Type)
Inspector, Aircraft Parts & Accessories
Instructor (Designated Specialty)
Instrument Mechanic, Aircraft
Investigator
Inventory Clerk
Key Punch Operator
Laundry Machine Operator
Legal Clerk
Library Clerk
Link Celestial Navigation Training Operator
Link Trainer Instructor
Link Trainer Mechanic
Machine Operator
Machinist
Maintenance Man, General
Materiel Clerk, Aviation
Meat Cutter
Mechanic, Aircraft (Designated Type)
Mechanic, Gunner, Aviation
Message Center Chief
Message Center Man
Messenger
Mess Sergeant
Metal smith, Aviation
Microfilm Technician
Military Policemen
Military Specialty Undetermined
Motor Transport
Multilith or Multigraph Operator
Navy Supply Man
Occupational Technician
Office Machine Repairman (Designated Machine)
Officer Candidate
Operations Clerk, Aviation
Orderly
Ordnance Stockman
Oxygen & Carbon Dioxide Man
Packer
Painter, Aircraft
Painter, General
Painter, Sign
Painter, Vehicle
Parachute Rigger
Parachute Shop Chief
Parts Clerk, Automotive
Parts Clerk, Ordnance
Passenger Transportation Clerk
Paymaster Clerk
Personnel Clerk
Photographer, Aerial
Photographer, Still
Photographic Darkroom Man
Photographic Laboratory Technician
Photographic Service Technician
Photographic Stock Man
Photolithographer
Photostat Operator or Blue Printer
Plastic Glass Worker
Platoon Sergeant
Plotter, Air Warning
Plumber
Police NCO
Postal Clerk
Post Exchange Man
Process Cameraman
Procurement Clerk
Projectionist, 16mm
Projectionist, 35mm
Projector Operator-repairman
Proofreader
Propeller Mechanic (Designated Type)
Property NCO
Printer
Publication Man
Quartermaster Supply Basic
Quartermaster Supply Man
Radar Operator (Designated Equipment)

Radar Repairman, Airborne Search Equipment
Radar Technician (Designated Equipment)
Radio Operator, Aerial
Radio Operator, High Speed
Radio Operator, Low Speed
Radio Repairman
Radio Technician, VHF
Radio Telephone Operator
Railway Clerk
Recognition Instructor
Recruiter
Recreation Assistant
Rigger, Aircraft
Sales Clerk
Sewing Machine Operator
Sergeant Major
Sheet Metal Worker
Ship Loading Man
Ship Clerk or Engineer Clerk, Aviation
Signal Stock Man
Small Arms Mechanic
Special Assignment Special Services Assistant Statistical Clerk Stenographer
Steward
Stock Clerk
Stock Man, General
Stock Record Clerk
Storage Battery Electrician
Student
Supply Records Clerk
Switchboard Installer, Telephone & Telegraph Dial
Switchboard Operator, Common Battery
Synthetic Devices Mechanic
Synthetic Gunnery Instructor (Designated Type)
Tabulation Machine Operator
Tailor
Telephone Switchboard Operator
Teletype Mechanic
Teletype Operator
Toolroom Keeper
Toxic Gas Handler
Tractor Driver
Traffic Rate Clerk
Training Aids Specialist
Translator (Designated Language)
Truck Driver, Heavy Truckmaster
Turret Mechanic Aircraft (Designated Type)
Upholsterer
Veterinary Technician
Warehouseman
Watch Repairman
Water Supply Man
Weather Forecaster
Weather Observer
Welder, Acetylene
Welder, Electric Arc
Woodworking Machine Operator
Truck Driver, Light or Chauffeur

APPENDIX 3
Buttons

<u>Officers</u>

Bronze 45 line – Officers	Overcoat fastening
Bronze 27 line – Officers	Overcoat shoulder straps
Bronze 40 line – Officers	Winter service coat fastening
Bronze 27 line – Officers	Winter service coat pockets and shoulder straps
Gilt 27 line – Officers	Summer dress coat / Shoulder straps Summer dress 'A'
Gilt 40 line – Officers	Fastening Summer dress 'A'
White pearl or bone	Summer service coat (1943-44)
Green buttons 25 line	Summer service & summer service (LS) pockets & shoulder straps (1945)
Green buttons 35 line	Summer service & summer service (LS) fastening (1945)
Bronze button 27 line – Officers	Winter service cap / Summer service cap
Gilt button 27 line – Officers	Summer dress cap

<u>Enlisted</u>

Bronze 45 line – Enlisted	Overcoat fastening
Bronze 25 line – Enlisted	Overcoat shoulder straps
Bronze 35 line – Enlisted	Winter service coat fastening
Bronze 25 line – Enlisted	Winter service coat pockets & shoulder straps
Gilt 25 line – Enlisted	Summer dress coat / Summer dress cap
Bronze 25 line – Enlisted	Winter service cap / Summer service cap
White pearl or bone	Summer service coat (1943–44)
Green buttons 25 line	Summer service & summer service (LS) pockets & shoulder straps (1945)
Green buttons 35 line	Summer service & summer service (LS) fastening (1945)

OFFICERS

Uniform item	Bronze 27 line	Bronze 40 line	Bronze 45 line
Overcoat fastening			✓
Overcoat shoulder straps	✓		
Winter service coat fastening		✓	
Winter service coat pockets & shoulder straps	✓		
Summer dress coat			
Shoulder straps Summer dress A			
Fastening Summer dress A			
Summer service coat (1943–44)			
Summer service & summer service (LS) pockets & shoulder straps (1945)			
Summer service & summer service (LS) fastening (1945)			
Winter service cap	✓		
Summer service cap	✓		
Summer dress cap			

	Gilt 27 line	Gilt 40 line	White pearl or bone	Green 25 line	Green 35 line
	✓				
	✓				
		✓			
			✓		
				✓	
					✓

BUTTONS

ENLISTED

Uniform item	Bronze 25 line	Bronze 35 line	Bronze 45 line
Overcoat fastening			✓
Overcoat shoulder straps	✓		
Winter service coat fastening		✓	
Winter service coat pockets & shoulder straps	✓		
Summer dress coat			
Summer dress cap			
Summer service coat (1943-44)			
Summer service & summer service (LS) pockets & shoulder straps (1945)			
Summer service & summer service (LS) fastening (1945)			
Winter service cap	✓		
Summer service cap	✓		

	Gilt 25 line	Gilt 40 line	White pearl or bone	Green 25 line	Green 35 line
	✓				
	✓				
			✓		
				✓	
					✓

APPENDIX 4
Memo to Lillian Sandy

```
1535-55-10
DHA-546-rlw
```

HEADQUARTERS
U. S. MARINE CORPS
WASHINGTON

11 January 1944

MEMORANDUM FOR MCWR ENLISTED PERSONNEL, CLASS VI(b):

Subject: General information and necessary equipment.

1. Until definite billets are assigned to you, use the following as your mailing address: - Recruit Depot, Marine Corps Women's Reserve Schools, Camp Lejeune, New River, North Carolina.

2. Do not arrive before the date specified in your orders. Do not leave home without orders and keep them with you at all times.

3. Bring essential clothing and toilet articles in a small bag which you can carry with you. Distribution of larger baggage may be delayed. All baggage must have a securely attached baggage tag, with your name plainly printed upon the tag.

4. Trunks are not allowed. You may have to carry your own baggage. Bear this in mind when packing.

5. Wear a pair of comfortable, low-heeled, dark brown laced oxfords. Have all personal possessions plainly marked.

6. Civilian clothes must be sent home as soon as uniforms are issued. You should bring enough clothes to last two weeks. Normally, summer uniforms will be issued to you within one week, and winter uniforms within two weeks after your arrival.

7. It is important to wear your hair simply and free of the collar. Headquarters, U. S. Marine Corps, Letter of Instruction #523--"Hair may touch, but shall not cover the coat collar."

8. It is important to dress warmly for traveling. There are unavoidable delays, frequently of some duration, in unheated train sheds.

9. <u>Necessary clothing.</u>

    (a) Rain coat and rain hat, if you possess these articles. (No umbrellas)
    (b) One suit and one additional skirt.
    (c) 4 or 5 blouses.
    (d) Plain bathrobe, or housecoat.
    (e) 1 pair soft-soled bedroom slippers.
    (f) Underwear, warm (vest and pants)
    (g) 1 pr. slacks, woolen. Slacks will be worn for organized physical training during winter months.
    (h) 2 pairs laced oxfords, dark brown, plain leather, plain or moccasin toe, heel not to exceed 12/8" (1½") in height. (A Third pair may be purchased during the training period, in the Uniform Shop on the Post.)
    (i) 1 pair rubbers or galoshes (black) to fit low-heeled oxfords.
    (j) 1 pair sneakers or rubber-soled shoes for physical training.
    (k) 2 pairs socks, woolen.
    (l) 1 Heavy coat.
    (m) 1 pr. Gloves.
    (n) 1 Sweater, slip-over, long-sleeve.

10. <u>Other required items:</u>

    (a) Travelers' checks for unforeseen personal expenses.
    (b) Name tags.
    (c) Stiff clothes brush.
    (d) 1 pair sun glasses.

11. You will be required to purchase the following articles after arrival at the Recruit Depot.

    (a) 1 Laundry Bag.
    (b) 1 box of Tissues.
    (c) 1 box of soap flakes.
    (d) 1 Toothpaste.
    (e) 1 Stationery Portfolio.
    (f) 1 Shoe Rag.
    (g) 1 Shoe Kit.
    (h) 1 Toothbrush.
    (i) 1 Soap Box.
    (j) 1 Toothbrush Holder.
    (k) 1 Plastic Cup.
    (l) 2 Pencils.
    (m) 1 Soap.
    (n) 1 Box sanitary napkins.
    (o) 1 Sewing Kit.
    (p) 12 Clothes Pins.
    (q) 1 Marine Handbook.
    (r) 1 Marking Set #1032.
    (s) 1 Name Stamp.
    (t) 3 Towels.
    (u) 2 Wash Cloths.
    (v) 1 Composition Book.

12. Uniforms.

You will be required to possess and maintain the following minimum articles of uniform, which are to be purchased after arrival at the Recruit Depot.

(a) 2 green uniforms, service, winter, enlisted
(b) 1 coat, trench.
(c) 1 handbag.
(d) 6 shirts, khaki.
(e) 1 cap, winter, enlisted.
(f) 6 neckties, khaki.
(g) 1 hat, summer, enlisted.
(h) 4 uniforms, summer.
(i) 1 cover, handbag, summer.
(j) 4 pair lisle hose.
(k) 1 pair gloves, dark brown, leather, short.
(l) 1 hat ornament, bronze.
(m) 2 collar ornaments, bronze.
(n) 1 hat ornament, gilt.
(o) 2 collar ornaments, gilt.
(p) 1 cap, summer, dress.
(q) 1 pair white gloves, cotton or rayon, short.

The following articles of uniform are optional:

(a) 1 muffler.
(b) 1 rain cap cover.
(c) 1 uniform, summer, dress.
(d) Pumps, white, with closed heel and toe, heel height not to exceed $20/8"$ ($2\frac{1}{2}"$), which may be worn off duty with white dress uniform.
(e) Pumps, plain dark brown leather, with closed toe, heel height not to exceed $20/8"$ ($2\frac{1}{2}"$), which may be worn off duty when not on duty with organized companies, with regular uniform.

-3-

13.   Two hundred dollars is available for uniforms upon assignment to active service. This allowance will be paid at the Recruit Depot.

14.   Luggage.

Since every recruit is issued a sea bag sufficient in size to accommodate all equipment, you will be permitted to retain for use, after you have completed your recruit training, only one suitcase not to exceed the 20" size. All other baggage must be returned home with your civilian clothes.

15.   The enclosed two shoe certificates may be used by you to purchase oxfords. These certificates, when used, shall be endorsed on the reverse side by the person to whom issued. If they are not used within thirty (30) days from the date of issue, they shall be turned over to your Commanding Officer to be forwarded to the Officer Procurement Division, Headquarters U. S. Marine Corps, Washington, D. C. In the event you do not attend indoctrination school, these certificates are to be returned by you to the above address.

CLARK W. THOMPSON,
Colonel, U. S. Marine Corps,
Officer in Charge, Officer Procurement Division,
Procurement Branch, Personnel Department.

APPENDIX 5
Uniforms and Accessories, MCWR
Issues and Quantities Contracted

Article	Issues from September 1944 to 31 July 1945	Quantities contracted for a 2½ year supply and issue
Apron, bungalow, WR	8,000	20,000
Belt, coat, trench, WR	1,700	2,750
Blankets, wool light green, WR	7,000	DQP
Buckles, coat, trench	2,400	5,800
Buttons, white, SS coat, WR	347 gross	500 gross
Buttons, coat, trench, WR	222 gross	307 gross
Buttons, green, SS & SSLS coat, WR	6,167 gross	15,000 gross
Buttons, raincoat, lightweight, WR	35 gross	350 gross
Buttons, sewing	35 gross	500 gross
Buttons, shirt, khaki, WR	243 gross	600 gross
Buttons, suit, exercise	42 gross	315 gross
Cap, dress, summer, WR	13,000	40,000
Cap, garrison, summer, WR	37,000	65,000
Cap, garrison, utility, WR	33,000	53,000
Cap, machine operators, WR	4,000	8,000
Cap, messwomen, WR	4,000	10,000
Cap, service, winter, WR	13,000	40,000
Chevrons, summer, green, WR	165,000	164,000
Coat, trench, c/w liner & hood	5,000	13,000
Coat, trench, WR	2,500	10,000
Coat, utility, WR	26,000	44,000
Cords, cap, red, WR	30,000	60,000
Cords, cap, white, WR	28,000	55,000
Cover, handbag, cloth, green w/strap	21,000	30,000
Cover, rain, cap, WR	26,000	42,000
Culotte, utility, WR	7,500	16,000
Fastener, slide, 7 inch	8,000	11,000
Gloves, cotton, brown, WR	5,000	45,000
Gloves, cotton, white, WR	28,000	60,000
Handbag, leather, w/strap, WR	9,000	17,000
Hood, coat, trench, WR	900	1,200
Jacket, field, WR	7,400	20,000
Liner, coat, trench, WR	100	500
Muffler, rayon, white, WR	30,000	50,000
Muffler, wool, red, WR	25,000	67,000
Overalls, utility, WR	29,000	39,000

Overcoat, WR	--	25,000
Overshoes, Arctic, WR	800	5,000
Raincoat, lightweight, WR	20,000	33,000
Raincoat, parka type, WR	1,600	6,000
Scarf, service, khaki, WR	62,000	150,000
Shirt, cotton, khaki, WR	46,000	140,000
Shirt, utility, WR	5,500	36,000
Shoes, field, WR	3,100	11,000
Shoes, Oxford, brown, WR	9,300	11,000
Shoes, pump, brown, WR	15,000	75,000
Shoes, pump, white, WR	12,000	35,000
Skirt, service, winter, WR	3,500	11,000
Slack, covert, WR	17,000	28,000
Slack, utility, WR	4,978	5,000
Strap, handbag, cloth, green, WR	700	40,000
Strap, handbag, leather, WR	3,500	15,000
Suit, exercise, WR	8,500	21,000
Uniform, dress, summer, WR	16,000	30,000
Uniform, undress, summer, WR	8,000	45,000
Uniform, service, summer, plisse, WR	38,000	43,000
Uniform, service, summer, seersucker, WR	3,000	45,000
Uniform, service, winter, WR	14,000	45,000
Vest, alpaca pile lined, WR	2,700	11,500

Miscellaneous

Heels	20,000	175,000
Soles	23,000	75,000
Rubber soling	96 sheets	2,100 sheets
Protectors, chest, plastic		150

Repair parts for handbag

Facile frame assemblies	3,400	50,000
Snap buttons	3,000	63,000
Tabs, leather	2,000	93,000

APPENDIX 6
Uniforms and Accessories, MCWR
Required Items

Item	(Retail outlet) Old unit price	(Quartermaster) New unit price
Uniform, service winter, WR	$28.05	$20.50
Uniform, dress, summer, WR	7.00	5.09
Uniform, undress, summer, WR	--	7.82
Uniform, service, summer, plisse, WR	6.55	4.83
Cap, service, winter, WR	5.95	2.80
Cap, dress, summer, WR	5.00	2.55
Cap, garrison, summer, WR	2.73	1.22
Buttons, green, SS & SSLS coat, WR	--	.30 set
Shirt, cotton, khaki, WR	2.67	1.87
Gloves, cotton, brown, WR	2.00*	1.00
Gloves, cotton, white, WR	2.00*	1.00
Handbag, leather, w/strap, WR	9.70	8.07
Cover, handbag, cloth, green, w/strap, WR	2.35	.60
Shoes, pump, brown, WR	6.50*	4.50
Shoes, pump, white, WR	6.50*	4.50
Shoes, Oxford, brown, WR	6.50*	4.15
Stockings, cotton, beige, WR	1.50*	.55
Stockings, rayon, beige, WR	1.50*	.64
Ornaments, cap-hat, bronze or plastic	.06	.06
Ornaments, cap-hat, gilt	.07	.07
Ornaments, collar, bronze or plastic	.08 pair	.08 pair
Ornaments, collar, bronze or plastic, left	.04	.04
Ornaments, collar, gilt	.10 pair	.10 pair
Coat, trench, complete with liner and hood, WR	38.00	25.82
Muffler, wool, red, WR	.61	.50
Muffler, rayon, white, WR	--	.58
Suit, exercise, WR	4.25	4.32
Cover, rain, cap, WR	2.20	1.51
Scarf, service, khaki, WR	.35	.24
TOTAL	$142.26	$105.31

*Estimated cost of purchase

Uniforms and Accessories, MCWR
Optional Items

Item	Old unit price	New unit price
Apron, mess	$.16	$.31
Bag, clothing	1.49	1.31
Band, official mourning	.28	.21
Cap, wool, knit, enlisted men's	.69	.69
Drawers, wool	1.37	1.39
Gloves, leather, lined, enlisted men's	1.53	1.56
Socks, wool	.26	.29
Undershirt, cotton	.26	.26
Undershirt, wool	1.37	1.46
Apron, bungalow, WR	2.49	2.49
Apron, office, khaki	.48	.48
Cap, garrison, utility, WR	.61	.82
Cap, machine operators, WR	.86	.71
Coat, utility, WR	2.38	2.19
Jacket, field, WR	8.04	8.22
Overall, utility, WR	2.83	2.83
Overshoes, arctic, WR	2.00	2.07
Raincoat, parka type, WR	6.64	6.64
Shoes, field, WR	4.51	4.51
Slacks, covert, WR	5.66	5.66
Vest, alpaca pile lined, WR	4.78	4.78

APPENDIX 7
Uniforms and Accessories, MCWR
List of Specifications

Article	Adopted	Revised	Amendment
Apron, bungalow, WR	27 May 44	Tentative	---------
Cap, dress, summer, WR	29 Jan 44	-------	-------
Cap, garrison, summer, WR	16 Jun 44	6 Sep 44	-------
Cap, garrison, utility, WR	22 Mar 44	------	-------
Cap, machine operators, WR	6 Jun 44	27 Sep 44 (8 Aug 45)	-------
Cap, messwomen, WR	23 Aug 44	(8 Aug 45)	-------
Cap, service, winter, WR	29 Jan 44	--------	--------
Coat, trench, complete with Liner and hood, WR	5 Oct 43	5 Dec 44	-------
Coat, utility, WR	2 Dec 43	(8 Aug 45)	8 Mar 45
Cover, cloth, green, w/strap, WR	1 May 44	2 Oct 44	-------
Cover, rain, cap, WR	6 Jun 44	23 Jun 44	-------
Culotte, utility, WR	30 Nov 44	-------	-------
Gloves, cotton, brown, WR			
Gloves, cotton, white, WR	7 Nov 44	-------	-------
Handbag, leather, w/strap, WR	1 May 44	-------	-------
Jacket, field, WR	17 May 44	6 Jun 44 / 5 Mar 45	-------
Muffler, rayon, white, WR	9 May 45	-------	-------
Muffler, wool, red, WR	4 Apr 44	-------	-------
Overall, utility, WR	8 Dec 43	26 Jul 44	-------
Overcoat, WR	17 Apr 45	-------	26 Jun 45
Overcoat, Officers, WR	7 Sep 43	-------	---------
Raincoat, lightweight, WR	12 Jun 44 (Modification – 15 Aug 44)	18 Aug 44	28 May 45
Scarf, service, khaki, WR	11 May 44	---------	---------
Shirt, cotton, khaki, WR	9 Dec 45	3 Jun 44 / 27 Jun 45	---------
Shirt, utility, WR	16 Nov 44	--------	---------
Shoes, pump, brown, WR			
Shoes, pump, white, WR	2 Oct 44 (tentative)	---------	
Slack, covert, WR	9 Jun 44	24 Jul 44 / 13 Dec 44	---------
Slack, utility, WR	28 Sep 44	Tentative	---------
Stockings, cotton, beige, WR	11 Jan 45	---------	5 Jul 45
Stockings, rayon, beige, WR	11 Jan 45	---------	5 Jul 45
Suit, exercise, WR	27 May 44	28 Dec 44	---------

Uniform, dress, summer, WR			
Coat	24 Apr 44	10 Apr 45	--------
Skirt	24 Apr 44	10 Apr 45	--------
Uniform, dress, summer A, Officers, WR			
Coat	2 Feb 44	---------	--------
Skirt	2 Feb 44	---------	--------
Uniform, service, summer, WR			
Coat	19 Feb 44	18 Jan 45	--------
Skirt	19 Feb 44	15 Jan 45	--------
Uniform, service, winter, WR			
Coat	10 Dec 43	29 May 45	--------
Skirt	11 Dec 43	29 May 45	--------
Uniform, undress, summer, WR			
Coat (service, summer LS)	18 Jan 45	---------	9 Jul 45
Skirt (service, summer)	19 Feb 44	15 Jan 45	---------
Vest, alpaca pile lined, WR	4 May 44	17 Nov 44	---------

APPENDIX 8
Uniform Regulations 1943

APPENDIX 9
Uniform Regulations 1945

UNIFORM REGULATIONS
U.S. MARINE CORPS WOMEN'S RESERVE
1943

HEADQUARTERS U.S. MARINE CORPS
WASHINGTON 25, D.C.

APPOROVED: 27 JULY 1943

JAMES FORRESTAL

SECRETARY OF THE NAVY

Revised 27 July 1943

UNIFORM REGULATIONS
UNITED STATES MARINE CORPS WOMEN'S RESERVE, 1943

CHAPTER I
GENERAL REGULATIONS

1. Uniform regulations, United States Marine Corps Women's Reserve, 1943, are published for the information and guidance of all officers and enlisted women of the Marine Corps Women's Reserve, who shall wear only the articles of uniform and equipment which are prescribed herein for their respective ranks and grades.

2. Articles corresponding to those prescribed may be substituted when necessary, in conformity with the Tables of Uniforms (Chapter VII). Additional articles which are required, or articles which are to be omitted, should be specified accordingly when prescribing a uniform. Parts of one uniform shall not be worn with parts of another except as authorized in these regulations, and so far as practicable, officers and enlisted women shall wear corresponding articles of the uniform when on duty together.

3. The uniform for officers and enlisted women for the day or for any particular occasion shall be fixed, if at a post or station, by the commanding officer of Marines or, if serving with the Navy, by the senior naval officer present with due regard to the duty to be performed and the state of the weather.

4. Officers and enlisted personnel shall wear the prescribed uniform at all times when appearing in public, except when engaged in active sports.

5. No pins or other jewelry shall be worn exposed upon the uniform by any officer or enlisted woman except authorized decorations, medals, badges and ribbons. A wrist watch and identification bracelet may be worn. Rings shall be inconspicuous.

6. Neatness and good grooming are of the utmost importance, slips shall not show below the uniform skirt. Stockings shall be worn right side out and the seams shall be straight. The cap shall be worn without tilting it to one side. Hair may touch but shall not cover the coat collar.

7. Clothes made by the women for themselves, made by tailors for them, or received by them from other than official sources shall conform strictly in material, pattern and making to the standard uniforms approved by the U.S. Marine Corps.

8. An umbrella is considered a non-military item and should not be carried by either officers or enlisted personnel when in uniform.

9. Commanding officers may authorize a member of the Marine Corps Women's Reserve to wear civilian dress, if she is a member of a wedding party.

10. No flowers shall be worn by any officer or enlisted woman of the Marine Corps while in uniform.

CHAPTER II
SPECIAL REGULATIONS

20. <u>Band, Official Mourning</u>
    Band, official mourning, to be fine quality black silk elastic jersey cloth, 3-1/4 inches wide. Band to be securely joined in center by being stitched with black silk thread and to measure, lying flat, 3-1/4 inches in width by 4-1/4 inches in length, width becoming approximately 3 inches when stretched on sleeve. To have two small black safety pins for fastening to sleeve.

21. <u>Buttons</u>
    (a) Buttons, bronze, will be worn by all personnel on winter dress and winter service uniforms.
    (b) Buttons, gilt, 27 line, officers, will be worn by officers on summer dress uniform.
    (c) Buttons, gilt, 25 line, enlisted, will be worn by enlisted personnel on summer dress uniform.
    (d) Buttons, white pearl or bone, will be worn by all personnel on summer service uniforms.
    (e) Buttons, gilt, officers, should be worn on the officers summer dress A coat, 40 line on the front and 27 line on shoulder straps.

22. <u>Cap</u>
    (a) Caps shall be worn under conditions when they would be worn in civil life.
    (b) A rain cover may be worn to protect the cap in inclement weather.

23. <u>Coat</u>
    (a) Winter service coats may be removed indoors by all personnel while engaged in office work.
    (b) When climatic conditions make it advisable, the commanding officer may prescribe the khaki shirt without the winter service coat.

24. <u>Galoshes, Boots and Rubbers</u>
    Plain black galoshes, boots or rubbers are required for all personnel and must fit Oxfords.

25. <u>Gloves</u>
    (a) Gloves will be worn under conditions when they would be worn in civil life.
    (b) Gloves, brown, will be short, leather or fabric, of commercial dark russet, dark brown mahogany or Cordovan color, with or without plain stitching of same color on back, lined or unlined, button, snap fastener, pull-on or buckle type.
    (c) Gloves, white, will be short, cotton or rayon, of plain design.

26. <u>Handbag</u>
(a) Handbag will be dark brown, buffalo leather, with dark brown shoulder strap of same material.
(b) Handbag strap may be worn either over or under the shoulder strap of coats or overcoat.
(c) With summer dress, summer dress A or summer service uniform, the light green summer cover and light green strap will be worn on the handbag.

27. <u>Handkerchiefs</u>
Handkerchiefs may be of khaki color when khaki shirt is worn, otherwise they shall be plain white.

28. <u>Hose</u>
(a) Full-length beige hose shall be worn by all personnel at all times when in uniform, except when in work clothes.
(b) Lisle hose shall be worn by all personnel in ranks.
(c) Hose of silk, rayon or other material may be worn by all personnel while engaged in office work and when off duty.
(d) Mesh hose shall not be worn.

29. <u>Muffler</u>
Mufflers of scarlet woolen material may be worn only with overcoats or trench coats.

30. <u>Ornaments</u>
(a) Cap and collar ornaments, officers, <u>dress</u>, shall be worn by officers with summer dress and summer service B.
(b) Cap and collar ornaments, officers, <u>Service</u>, shall be worn by officers with summer service A, winter dress and winter service uniforms.
(c) Cap and collar, enlisted, dress, shall be worn by enlisted personnel with summer dress, summer service B and summer service C uniforms.
(d) Cap and collar, enlisted, service, shall be worn by enlisted personnel with winter service and summer service A uniforms.

31. <u>Overcoat</u>
Officers may wear overcoats off duty, and while on duty except in ranks.

32. <u>Scarf</u>
(a) Khaki color scarf, tied in four-in-hand knot, shall be worn with khaki shirt.
(b) Officers shall wear dark green scarf, tied in four-in-hand knot, with white shirt.

33. <u>Shirt</u>
(a) Small insignia of rank shall be worn by commissioned officers on the collar of khaki shirt, when service coat is not worn.
(b) Chevrons shall be worn on left sleeve only of khaki shirt by non-commissioned

officers and enlisted personnel.
(c) Khaki shirt, and khaki scarf tied in four-in-hand knot, shall be worn by all personnel with winter service uniforms.
(d) White shirt, and dark green scarf tied in four-in-hand knot, may be worn by officers with winter dress uniform when off duty.
(e) Shirts shall not be worn with summer dress and summer service uniforms. White blouse shall be worn with summer dress A uniform.

34. <u>Shoes</u>
(a) Leather Oxfords of plain design, of commercial dark russet, dark brown mahogany, or Cordovan color, heels not to exceed 1-1/2 inches in height, shall be worn by all personnel in ranks. Suede shoes are not permitted.
(b) Plain leather pumps of commercial dark russet, dark brown mahogany or Cordovan color, with closed toes and heels, a flat bow and heels not exceeding 2-1/2 inches in height may be worn by all personnel while engaged in office work and when off duty.
(c) White pumps, leather, plain design, with closed toes and heels, a flat bow and heels not exceeding 2-1/2 inches in height shall be worn by all personnel with summer dress uniform.
(d) White pumps shall be worn by all personnel with summer service uniform while on procurement duty and may be worn off duty.

35. <u>Skirts</u>
The length of the skirt shall be at least to the turn of the calf.

36. <u>Sports Clothing</u>
(a) Bathing suits may be of preferred color but shall not be extreme in cut.
(b) Slacks or shorts may be worn only when actually engaged in sports that would require them in civil life. A skirt shall be worn over shorts on the way to and from sports areas.

37. <u>Trench Coat and Raincoat, Lightweight</u>
(a) Trench coat shall be worn by all personnel in ranks when appropriate.
(b) Trench coat may be worn as an overcoat by all personnel.
(c) Officers may wear lightweight raincoats off duty and while on duty, except in ranks.

38. <u>Work clothes</u>
Work clothes will be provided and issued as organizational equipment. The commanding officer shall prescribe the personnel who shall wear work clothes and the times and places when they shall be worn.

CHAPTER III
ARTICLES OF THE UNIFORM FOR OFFICERS

50. Unless otherwise ordered, offices of the Marine Corps Women's Reserve shall provide themselves with the articles indicated for their respective ranks, as follows:

Band, official, mourning
Blouse, dress, summer A
Buttons, bronze
Buttons, gilt
Buttons, white pearl or bone
Cap, dress, and service, summer
Cap, garrison summer. Authorized but not required. The left service collar ornament shall be worn on the left side of cap; garrison and the small insignia of rank shall be placed on the right side, directly opposite the left service collar ornament.
Cap, service, winter
Coat, dress, summer
Coat, dress, summer A
Coat, service, summer
Coat, service, winter
Coat, trench
Cover, cap, rain. Authorized but not required
Cover, handbag and strap, summer
Galoshes, boots or rubbers
Gloves, brown
Gloves, white
Handbag
Hose
Insignia of rank
Miniatures of decorations and medals. Authorized but not required
Muffler, authorized but not required
Ornament, cap, dress
Ornament, cap, service
Ornament, collar service, left. Authorized but not required
Ornaments, collar, dress
Ornaments, collar, service
Overcoat, authorized but not required
Raincoat, lightweight. Authorized but not required
Scarf, dress, dark green
Scarf, service, khaki
Shirt, khaki

Shirt, white
Shoes, brown, Oxfords
Shoes, brown, pumps
Shoes, white, pumps
Shoulder straps, summer, green
Skirt, dress, summer
Skirt, dress, summer A
Skirt, service, summer
Skirt, service, winter
Sports clothing, authorized but not required.

CHAPTER IV
OCCASION ON WHICH EACH UNIFORM IS TO BE WORN

60. When on duty, or attending ceremonies or social functions in an official capacity, officers shall wear the uniform prescribed for the occasion or as ordered by the senior officer present. Officers attending functions at the White House should consult Headquarters Marine Corps, which will prescribe the appropriate uniform for the occasion and season. In prescribing a uniform other than service, due consideration shall be given to the temperature and to the relative importance of the occasion in deciding whether the uniform should be green, green and white stripe, or white.

61. Winter dress, summer dress, summer dress A or summer service B may be prescribed for officers at all posts on social occasions, when not in line with troops and when off duty.

62. Winter dress, summer dress or summer service B shall be the uniforms for enlisted personnel off duty.

63. Summer service A or B at the discretion of the officer in charge of the procurement division, and winter service shall be the uniforms for officers on procurement duty, summer and winter respectively.

64. Summer service A or B at the discretion of the officer in charge of the procurement division, and winter service shall be the uniforms for enlisted personnel on procurement duty, summer and winter respectively.

65. Winter service and summer service A, for officers, and winter service and summer service C, for enlisted personnel, shall be the uniforms for parades, winter and summer respectively.

66. Winter service is prescribed as the duty uniform at all posts during the period of the year when heavy clothing is necessary.

67. Summer service A is prescribed as the duty uniform at all posts during the period of the year when light clothing is necessary.

CHAPTER V
INSIGNIA, ORNAMENTS, ETC
COMMISSIONED OFFICERS

INSIGNIA OF RANK

75. Officers shall wear the insignia of rank on the shoulder straps of all coats, except summer dress A, the overcoat and the trench coat on the center line of each shoulder strap, with the outer edge of insignia ¾ inch from the armhole seam. On summer dress A coat, the insignia of rank shall be worn on the center line of each shoulder strap, equidistant between the button and the ornament (see plate No 2).

76.
(a) When coats are not worn with winter service uniforms, the small insignia of rank shall be worn on the collar of the khaki shirt, being centered on each side of the collar 1 inch from the front edge, with the collar turned down.
(b) On the garrison cap, the small insignia of rank shall be placed on the right side, directly opposite the left service collar ornament.

77. <u>Colonel</u> – on the shoulder strap, the head of the eagle shall be toward the collar end; on the garrison cap it shall be toward the top; and on the khaki shirt, toward the top of the collar, with the eagle in each case facing the front.

78. <u>Lieutenant Colonel and Major</u> – on the shoulder strap, the tip of the leaf shall point toward the collar end, on the garrison cap it shall point toward the top, and on the khaki shirt, toward the top of the collar.

79. <u>Captain</u> – the bars shall be worn with the long axis in a line from front to rear on the shoulder strap, in a vertical line on the garrison cap and parallel to the front edge of the collar on the khaki shirt.

80. <u>First Lieutenant and Second Lieutenant</u> – the bar shall be worn with the long axis in a line from front to rear on the shoulder strap, in a vertical line on the garrison cap and parallel to the front edge of the collar on the khaki shirt.

CAP ORNAMENTS

81. The service cap ornament shall be worn on the winter service cap and the summer dress cap with summer service A uniforms. The dress cap ornament shall be worn on the summer dress cap with summer dress, summer dress A and summer service B uniforms. On the garrison cap the left service collar ornament shall be worn on the left side, in the place provided therefor.

82.
(a) Service collar ornaments shall be worn on the winter service coat and summer service A coat, centered on the collar between the crease roll and outer edge with center of hemisphere 1 inch above the horizontal edge of lapel notch, the vertical axis of ornament being parallel with crease roll and eagle facing inside (see illustration No 1).
(b) Dress ornaments shall be worn on the summer dress and summer service B coats, centered on the collar at a point 3-1/4 inches from the point of the collar measuring along the outside edge and 1-3/4 inches from the outside edge measuring toward the notch, the vertical axis of ornament being parallel with crease roll and eagle facing inside (see illustration No 3).
(c) Dress collar ornaments shall be worn on the summer dress A coat on the center line of each shoulder strap, center of hemisphere ¾ inch from the armhole seam with head of eagle facing front (see plate No 2 (Revised)).

MISCELLANEOUS (OFFICERS)

83. Band, official mourning, shall be worn on the left arm above the elbow. This band may also be worn by officers as family mourning.

CHAPTER VI
CHEVRONS, ORNAMENTS, ETC
ENLISTED PERSONNEL

CHEVRONS

84. Chevrons shall be worn, points up, on the left sleeve of khaki shirt and all coats, except trench coat, midway between the elbow and armhole seam, in the center of the outer half of sleeve. Winter service chevrons shall be worn on the winter service coat; khaki chevrons on khaki shirts; and summer chevrons, green, on summer service and summer dress coats. Chevrons shall be worn as prescribed for men of like rank.

CAP ORNAMENTS

85. The service cap ornament shall be worn on the winter service cap and summer dress cap with summer service C uniform. The dress cap ornament shall be worn on the summer dress cap with summer dress and summer service B uniforms. On the garrison cap the left service collar ornament shall be worn in the left side, in the place provided therefor.

COLLAR ORNAMENTS

86.
(a) Service collar ornaments shall be worn on winter service coat, centered on the collar between the crease roll and outer edge with center of hemisphere 1 inch above the horizontal edge of lapel notch, the vertical axis of ornament at right angles to the horizontal edge of notch, with eagle facing inside (see illustration No 2).
(b) Dress collar ornaments shall be worn on summer dress coat and summer service B coat, and service collar ornaments on summer service A coat and summer service C coat, centered on the collar at a point 3-1/4 inches from point of the collar measuring along the outside edge and 1-3/4 inches from the outside edge measuring toward the notch, the vertical axis of ornament at right angles to the horizontal edge of notch, with eagle facing inside (see illustration No 4).

MISCELLANEOUS (ENLISTED WOMEN)

87. Band, official mourning, for pallbearers at military funerals only, to be worn on the left arm above the elbow, below chevron.

88. Band, sick list, shall be worn on the right sleeve midway between the shoulder seam and the elbow.

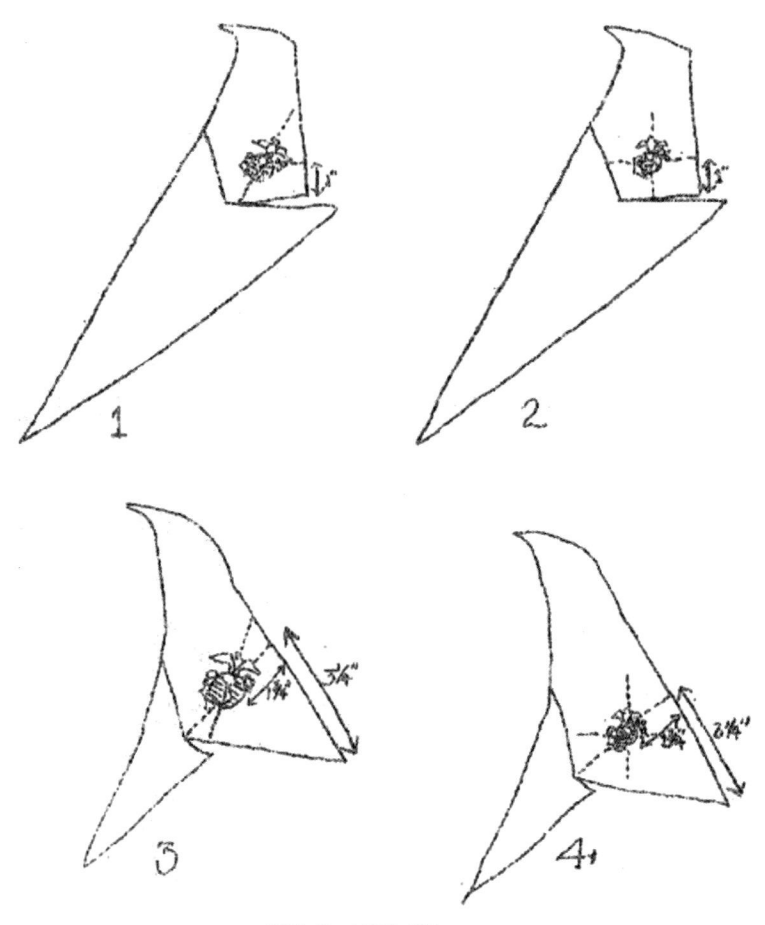

COLLAR ORNAMENTS

Nos. 1 - 3. Officers.
Nos. 2 - 4. Enlisted Women

Plate 1 – collar ornaments

CHAPTER VII – TABLES OF UNIFORMS
COMMISSIONED OFFICERS

UNIFORM	CAP	COAT	SKIRT	BUTTONS	SHIRT	SCARF
Winter dress	Green (1)	Green (1)	Green (1)	Bronze	White	Dark Green
Winter service	Green (1)	Green (1)	Green (1)	Bronze	Khaki	Khaki
Summer dress	Light Green (12)	White (9)	White (9)	Gilt	–	–
Summer dress A	Light Green (12)	White (9)	White (9)	Gilt	–	–
Summer service A	Light Green (12) Garrison (13)	Green & white stripe	Green & white stripe	White pearl	–	–
Summer service B	Light Green (12)	Green & white stripe	Green & white stripe	White pearl	–	–

(1) Forestry green serge or covert cloth, <u>or other suitable cloth of adopted standard</u>
(2) Pumps
(3) Silk, rayon or similar material
(4) Bronze
(5) Oxfords in ranks. Pumps may be worn while engaged in office work and when off duty
(6) Lisle in ranks, otherwise silk, rayon or similar material
(7) Trench coat in ranks
(9) Twill, tropical worsted, palm beach cloth or similar material
(10) Brown bag with light green cover and strap
(11) Gold and silver
(12) Spruce green with white cord
(13) Wearing optional
(14) Ribbons may be worn with service uniforms
(15) Miniature medals may be worn with dress uniforms
(16) Leather in ranks, otherwise leather or fabric
(17) Shoulder strap, summer, green
(18) Trench coat, overcoat, or lightweight raincoat. See paragraph 37
(19) Trench coat or lightweight raincoat. See paragraph 37

GLOVES	HANDBAG	SHOES	HOSE	ORNAMENTS	OUTER COAT
Brown (16)	Brown	Brown (2)	Beige (3)	Service (4)	(18)
Brown	Brown	Brown (5)	Beige (6)	Service (4)	(7)(18)
White	Green cover (10)	White (2)	Beige (3)	Dress (11)	(19)
White	Green cover (10)	White (2)	Beige (3)	Dress (11)	(19)
White (13)	Green cover (10)	Brown (5)	Beige (6)	Service (4)	(7)(19)
White	Green cover (10)	White (2)	Beige (3)	Dress (11)	(19)

CHAPTER VII – TABLES OF UNIFORMS
ENLISTED PERSONNEL

UNIFORM	CAP	COAT	SKIRT	BUTTONS	SHIRT	SCARF
Winter dress	Green (1)	Green (1)	Green (1)	Bronze	Khaki	Khaki
Winter service	Green (1)	Green (1)	Green (1)	Bronze	Khaki	Khaki
Summer dress	Light Green (7)	White (8)	White (8)	Gilt	–	–
Summer service A	Garrison	Green & white stripe	Green & white stripe	White pearl	–	–
Summer service B	Light Green (7)	Green & white stripe	Green & white stripe	White pearl	–	–
Summer service C	Light Green (7)	Green & white stripe	Green & white stripe	White pearl	–	–

(1) Forestry green serge or covert cloth
(2) Pumps
(3) Silk, rayon or similar material
(4) Bronze
(5) Oxfords in ranks. Pumps may be worn by enlisted personnel engaged in office work and while off duty
(6) Lisle while in ranks
(7) Spruce green with white cord
(8) Twill
(9) Brown bag with green summer cover and green strap
(10) Gilt
(11) Wearing optional
(12) Oxfords
(13) Leather in ranks, otherwise leather or fabric
(14) Trench coat, or lightweight raincoat. See paragraph 37
(15) See paragraph 37

GLOVES	HANDBAG	SHOES	HOSE	ORNAMENTS	OUTER COAT
Brown (13)	Brown	Brown (2)	Beige (3)	Service (4)	(14)
Brown	Brown	Brown (5)	Beige (6)	Service (4)	(15)
White	Green cover (9)	White (2)	Beige (3)	Dress (10)	(14)
White (11)	Green cover (9)	Brown (5)	Beige (6)	Service (4)	(15)
White (11)	Green cover (9)	White (2)	Beige (3)	Dress (10)	(14)
White		Brown (12)	Beige (6)	Service (4)	(15)

UNIFORM REGULATIONS
U.S. MARINE CORPS WOMEN'S RESERVE
1945

HEADQUARTERS U.S. MARINE CORPS
WASHINGTON 25, D.C.

APPOROVED: 30 APRIL 1945

JAMES FORRESTAL

SECRETARY OF THE NAVY

2275-120
DB-311-mve

HEADQUARTERS U.S. MARINE CORPS
Washington

20 April 1945

From: Commandant of the Marine Corps
To: All Commanding Officers, Posts and Stations, within the United States, including Procurement Offices, and the Fourteenth Naval District.
All Officers, Marine Corps Women's Reerve.

Subject: Uniform Regulations, U.S. Marine Corps Women's Reserve, 1945

References: (a) Ltr of Instn No. 523, 27 Aug 1943, as modified by Ltrs of Instn Nos. 629, 670, 777, 803 and 955.
(b) Ltr of Instn No. 489, 16 July 1943.

Enclosure: (A) Copy of subject regulations.

1. The enclosed Uniform Regulations, U.S. Marine Corps Women's Reserve, 1945, are published for the information and guidance of all concerned. These regulations supersede Uniform Regulations, U.S. Marine Corps Women's Reserve, 1943, as published in reference (a).

2. Reference (a) and paragraph 3(h) of reference (b) are hereby revoked.

D PECK

Acting

APPROVED: 30 April 1945

JAMES FORRESTAL
Secretary of the Navy

TABLE OF CONTENTS

			Page
Chapter	I	General Regulations	1
	II	Special Regulations	3
	III	Occasions on which each uniform is to be worn	7
	IV	Insignia, Ornaments etc., Commissioned Officers:	
		Insignia of Rank	8
		Cap Ornaments	9
		Collar Ornaments	9
		Miscellaneous (Officers)	10
	V	Chevrons, Ornaments, etc., Enlisted Personnel:	
		Chevrons	10
		Cap Ornaments	10
		Collar Ornaments	11
		Miscellaneous (Enlisted Women)	11
	VI	Decorations, Medals, Ribbons and Badges	11
	VII	Tables of Uniforms:	
		Commissioned Officers	12
		Enlisted Personnel	13
		Index	14
		List of Illustrations	17

UNIFORM REGULATIONS
UNITED STATES MARINE CORPS WOMEN'S RESERVE, 1945

CHAPTER I
GENERAL REGULATIONS

1. Uniform Regulations, United States Marine Corps Women's Reserve, 1945, are published for the information of all officers of the United States Marine Corps and Marine Corps Reserve; and for the information and guidance of all officers and enlisted persons of the Marine Corps Women's Reserve, who shall wear only the articles of uniform, and accessories thereto, prescribed herein for their respective ranks.

2. Unless otherwise ordered, officers and enlisted persons shall provide themselves with the articles indicated herein; except that possession of the summer dress A uniform by officers and the lightweight raincoat by officers and enlisted persons, is optional.

3. Parts of one uniform shall not be worn with parts of another except as authorized in these regulations, or, in an emergency, as authorized by the commanding officer. So far as practicable, officers and enlisted persons shall wear corresponding articles of the uniform when on duty together.

4. The uniform to be worn for the season, day or occasion shall be prescribed by the commanding officer with due regard to the duty to be performed and the state of the weather.

5. Officers and enlisted persons shall wear the prescribed uniform at all times when appearing in public, except while engaged in work or active sports which require special clothing.

6. The uniform of the day for officers and enlisted persons shall be posted on a bulletin board and a copy of these regulations shall be placed where they may be consulted.

7. Outer clothing worn by officers and enlisted persons shall conform to applicable specifications and/or these regulations. Should an emergency render it necessary temporarily to wear clothing that does not conform to specifications and/or regulations, such clothing shall conform as nearly as possible and shall be carefully inspected by the commanding officer before being worn.

8. Commanding officers will inspect and verify service uniforms and work clothes

of the persons under their command as often as may be necessary to ensure that all members thereof are properly equipped with those articles necessary for performance of the particular duty involved.

9. Unless otherwise specified, changes in these regulations and in specifications of uniforms will become effective upon publication.

10. Officers suspended from duty by sentence of a court martial are prohibited from wearing the uniform during such period.

11. Officers shall maintain their uniforms in a thoroughly near and serviceable condition and shall, by their appearance, set an example of neatness and strict conformity to Uniform Regulations.

12. Enlisted persons shall be neat and trim in person and dress on all occasions, and commanding officers will be held responsible at all times for the appearance of persons serving under them. Officers, and commanding officers especially, will impress upon the enlisted persons that the dignity of the uniform and the respect due it are best preserved when its wearer so conducts herself as never to cast discredit upon it. Careful inspection of uniforms shall be made before enlisted persons go on liberty. All officers will observe the appearance of enlisted persons on liberty or furlough and will report those that may be out of uniform or in an untidy condition.

13. Commanding officers shall exercise close supervision over the fitting of uniforms of enlisted persons, shall encourage them to keep their uniforms clean and neat, and shall do everything possible to facilitate the proper care, cleaning and preservation of uniforms.

14. No pins or other jewellery shall be worn exposed upon the uniform by any officer or enlisted person except authorized decorations, medals, badges and ribbons. A wrist-watch and identification bracelet may be worn. Rings shall be inconspicuous.

15. An umbrella is considered a non-military item and shall not be carried by officers or enlisted persons.

16. Commanding officers may authorize a member of the Marine Corps Women's Reserve to wear civilian dress if she is a member of a wedding party, i.e. bride, bridesmaid or attendant.

17. Clothes made by tailors for women reservists, or received from other than official sources, shall conform strictly in material, pattern and make to the standard uniforms approved herein. (See Chapter VII)

18. No flowers shall be worn by any officer or enlisted person while in uniform.

CHAPTER II
SPECIAL REGULATIONS

30. <u>Band, official mourning</u>
    The official mourning band shall be of fine quality black elastic jersey cloth, 3-1/4 inches wide. The band shall be securely joined in the center by being stitched with black thread, and shall measure, lying flat, 3-1/4 inches in width by 4-1/4 inches in length, width becoming approximately 3 inches when stretched on sleeve. The band shall have two small black safety pins for fastening to the sleeve.

31. <u>BUTTONS</u>
    (a) Bronze buttons shall be worn by all personnel on the winter dress and winter service uniforms.
    (b) Gilt buttons, 27 line, officers, shall be worn by officers on the summer dress coat.
    (c) Gilt buttons, 25 line, enlisted, shall be worn by enlisted persons on the summer dress coat.
    (d) Green buttons, 25 line on pockets and shoulder straps and 35 line on front of coat, shall be worn by all personnel on the summer service and summer service LS (long sleeve) coats.
    (e) Gilt buttons, officers, 27 line on the shoulder straps, and 40 line on front of coat, shall be worn on the summer dress A coat.
    (f) Bronze buttons, 27 line, shall be worn by officers on the summer dress cap when the service ornament is worn. Gilt buttons, 27 line, officers, shall be worn by officers on the summer dress cap when the dress ornament is worn.
    (g) Bronze buttons, 25 line, shall be worn by enlisted persons on the summer dress cap when the bronze ornament is worn, and gilt buttons, 25 line, enlisted, when the gilt ornament is worn.
    (h) Uniform garments shall be properly buttoned at all times when worn.

32. <u>CAP</u>
    (a) The appropriate cap shall be worn with the uniform out of doors.
    (b) The cap may be removed indoors when considered appropriate.
    (c) The authorized cap cover may be worn in inclement weather.

33. <u>COAT</u>
    The coat shall be worn with the winter uniform at all times except as otherwise prescribed by the commanding officer.

34. <u>GALOSHES, BOOTS AND RUBBERS</u>
    Plain black galoshes, boots or rubbers, to fit Oxfords, are required for all personnel.

35. <u>GLOVES</u>
(a) Brown gloves shall be short, leather or fabric, of commercial dark russet, dark brown mahogany or Cordovan color, of plain design, with or without plain stitching of same colour on back, lined or unlined, button, snap fastener, pull-on or buckle type.
(b) White gloves shall be short, cotton or rayon, of plain design.
(c) Brown gloves shall be worn at all times with the winter dress and service uniforms.
(d) White gloves shall be worn at all times with the summer uniform, except that with the summer service uniform, gloves are optional.
(e) Gloves may be removed indoors.

36. <u>GROOMING</u>
(a) Lipstick, if worn, shall harmonize with the color of the winter service cap cord and shall be neatly and thinly applied.
(b) Rouge, mascara, and hair tints, if used, shall be inconspicuous.
(c) Colored nail polish, if worn, shall harmonize with the color of the winter service cap cord.
(d) Hair may touch but not cover the collar.
(e) Slips shall be worn with all uniforms.
(f) Slips shall not show below the uniform skirt.

37. <u>HANDBAG</u>
(a) The leather handbag, with the appropriate strap, shall be worn with all uniforms, except for parades. The green cover shall be on the handbag when summer uniforms are worn.
(b) The handbag strap may be worn either over or under the shoulder strap of coats.

38. <u>HANDKERCHIEFS</u>
Handkerchiefs may be khaki color when khaki shirt is worn, otherwise they shall be plain white.

39. <u>HOSE</u>
(a) Full length beige hose shall be worn by all personnel at all times when in uniform.
(b) Lisle hose shall be worn by all personnel in ranks. (This requirement may be modified by the commanding officer if compliance is inconsistent with paragraph 39 (c))
(c) Hose of silk, rayon, or nylon may be worn by all personnel while engaged in office work and when off duty.
(d) Mesh or seamless hose shall not be worn.
(e) Hose shall be worn with the seams straight.

40. <u>JACKET, FIELD</u>
Field jackets may be worn while on a post or station with the winter service skirt at the discretion of the commanding officer.

41. MUFFLERS
(a) The red wool muffler shall be worn with the overcoat, trench coat and lightweight raincoat with the winter uniforms.
(b) The white rayon muffler shall be worn with the trench coat and lightweight raincoat with the summer uniforms.

42. ORNAMENTS
(a) Cap and collar ornaments, officers, dress, shall be worn by officers with the summer dress and summer dress A uniforms, and with the summer undress uniform when white pumps are worn.
(b) Cap and collar ornaments, officers, service, shall be worn by officers with the winter dress, winter service, summer service, and summer parade uniforms and with the summer undress uniform when brown pumps are worn.
(c) Cap and collar ornaments, enlisted, gilt, shall be worn by enlisted persons with summer dress and summer undress uniforms.
(d) Cap and collar ornaments, enlisted, bronze, shall be worn by enlisted persons with the winter dress, winter service, summer service and summer parade uniforms.

43. OVERCOAT
(a) Officers and enlisted persons may wear the overcoat off duty, and while on duty at the discretion of the commanding officer.

44. SCARFS
(a) The khaki service scarf, tied in four-in-hand knot, shall be worn with khaki shirt.
(b) Officers shall wear the green dress scarf, tied in four-in-hand knot, with white shirt.

45. SHOES
(a) Smooth leather Oxfords of plain design, of commercial dark russet, dark brown mahogany or Cordovan color, with heels not to exceed 1-1/2 inches in height, shall be worn by all personnel in ranks.
(b) Smooth leather pumps of commercial dark russet, dark brown mahogany or Cordovan color, with closed toes and heels, with a flat bow and heels not exceeding 2-1/2 inches in height, may be worn as indicated in Chapter VII.
(c) White pumps, leather, plain design, with closed toes and heels, with a flat bow and heels not exceeding 2-1/2 inches in height shall be worn as indicated in Chapter VII.

46. SKIRTS
(a) Skirts and outer coats shall extend to bottom of kneecaps when the individual is in standing position.
(b) Seams in skirts shall be pressed open and flat, never creased.

47. SPORTS CLOTHING

(a) Bathing suits may be of preferred color but shall not be extreme in cut.
(b) Covert slacks, utility slacks, shorts, culottes, utility shirts, field jackets or exercise suits, in appropriate combinations, may be worn when actually engaged in sports that would require them in civilian life, at the discretion of the commanding officer. A skirt shall be worn over shorts on way to and from sports area.
(c) Field jackets may be worn for sports with slacks, culottes and winter service skirt at the discretion of the commanding officer.

48. TRENCH COAT, OVERCOAT AND LIGHTWEIGHT RAINCOAT
(a) The trench coat or overcoat shall be worn with winter uniforms, at the discretion of the commanding officer, by all personnel in ranks.
(b) The trench coat shall be worn with summer uniforms, at the discretion of the commanding officer, by all personnel in ranks.
(c) Officers and enlisted persons may wear lightweight raincoats off duty; and while on duty at the discretion of the commanding officer.

49. WORK CLOTHES
(a) Work clothes issued or sold by the Quartermaster's Department are for wear by enlisted persons, as prescribed by the commanding officer.

CHAPTER III
OCCASIONS ON WHICH EACH UNIFORM IS TO BE WORN

60. When on duty, or attending ceremonies or social functions in an official capacity, officers shall wear the uniform prescribed for the occasion or as ordered by the senior officer present. Officers attending functions at the White House should consult Headquarters Marine Corps, which will prescribe the appropriate uniform for the occasion and season. In prescribing a uniform, due consideration shall be given to the temperature and to the relative importance of the occasion.

61. Appropriate uniforms may be prescribed by the commanding officer for officers and enlisted persons for social occasions, when not in line with troops, and when off duty.

62. Summer service or summer undress, at the discretion of the Officer in Charge of the Procurement Division, and winter service, shall be the uniforms for officers on procurement duty, summer and winter respectively.

63. Summer service or summer undress, at the discretion of the Officer in Charge of the Procurement Division, and winter service, shall be the uniforms for enlisted persons on procurement duty, summer and winter respectively.

64. Winter service and summer parade shall be the uniforms for parades for all personnel, winter and summer respectively.

65. Winter service is prescribed as the duty uniform at all posts during the period of the year when heavy clothing is necessary.

66. Summer service is prescribed as the duty uniform at all posts during the period of the year when light clothing is necessary.

CHAPTER IV
INSIGNIA, ORNAMENTS, ETC
COMMISSIONED OFFICERS

INSIGNIA OF RANK

75. Officers shall wear the insignia of rank on all uniform coats (except summer dress A) the overcoat, the lightweight raincoat, the trench coat and the field jacket, on the center line of each shoulder strap, with the outer edge of insignia ¾ inch from the armhole seam. On summer dress A coat, the insignia of rank shall be worn on the center line of each shoulder strap, equidistant between the button and the ornament (see Plate 2).

76. Officers shall wear detachable green shoulder straps over the regular shoulder straps of the summer dress, summer service and summer service LS coats. The pointed end of the shoulder strap shall be secured by means of the shoulder strap button. The outer end, which shall be in line with the armhole seam, may be sewed, or secured by the insignia of rank.

77.
(a) When uniform coats are not worn with winter service uniforms, the small insignia of rank shall be worn on the collar of the khaki shirt, centered on each side of the collar 1 inch from the front edge, with the collar turned down.
(b) On the garrison cap, the small insignia of rank shall be placed on the right side, directly opposite the left service collar ornament.

79. <u>Colonel</u> – on the shoulder strap, the head of the eagle shall be toward the collar, on the garrison cap it shall be toward the top, and on the khaki shirt, toward the top of the collar, with the eagle in each case facing the front.

80. <u>Lieutenant Colonel and Major</u> – on the shoulder strap, the tip of the leaf shall point toward the collar, on the garrison cap it shall point toward the top and on the khaki shirt toward the top of the collar.

81. <u>Captain</u> – the bars shall be worn with the long axis in a line from front to rear on the shoulder strap, in a vertical line on the garrison cap and parallel to the front edge of the collar on the khaki shirt.

82. <u>First Lieutenant and Second Lieutenant</u> – the bar shall be worn with the long axis in a line from front to rear on the shoulder strap, in a vertical line on the garrison cap and parallel to the front edge of the collar on the khaki shirt.

CAP ORNAMENTS

83.
(a) The service cap ornament shall be worn on the winter service cap, and on the summer dress cap with summer service and summer parade uniforms, and with the summer undress uniform when brown pumps are worn.
(b) The dress cap ornament shall be worn on the summer dress cap with summer dress and summer dress A uniforms, and with the summer undress uniform when white pumps are worn.
(c) The left service collar ornament shall be worn on the garrison cap, on the left side, in the place provided therefor.
(d) The cap ornament shall be worn with eagle up.

COLLAR ORNAMENTS

84.
(a) Service collar ornaments shall be worn on the winter service coat centered on the collar between the crease roll and outer edge with center of hemisphere 1 inch above the horizontal edge of lapel notch, the vertical axis of ornament being parallel with crease roll and eagle facing inside (see Plate 1, illustration No. 1).
(b) Collar ornaments shall be worn on the summer dress, summer service, and summer service LS coats centered on the collar at a point 3-1/4 inches from the point of the collar measuring along the outside edge and 1-3/4 inches from the outside edge measuring toward the notch, the vertical axis of the ornament being parallel with crease roll and eagle facing inside (see Plate 1, illustration No 3).
(c) Dress collar ornaments shall be worn on the summer dress coat, and on the summer service LS coat, when the latter is worn with white pumps.
(d) Service collar ornaments shall be worn on the summer service coat, and on the summer service LS coat, when prescribed as summer parade uniform; also when the summer service LS coat is worn with brown pumps.
(e) Dress collar ornaments shall be worn on the summer dress A coat on the centre line of each shoulder strap, center of hemisphere 3/4 inch from the armhole seam with head of eagle facing front (See Plate 2).

MISCELLANEOUS (OFFICERS)

85. The official mourning band shall be worn on the left sleeve (fastened at back), midway between the armhole seam and the elbow. This band may also be worn by officers as family mourning.

CHAPTER V
CHEVRONS, ORNAMENTS, ETC
ENLISTED PERSONNEL

CHEVRONS
95. Chevrons shall be worn, points up, on both sleeves of the khaki shirt, field jacket, and all coats, except the trench coat and lightweight raincoat, midway between the elbow and armhole seam, in the center of the outer half of the sleeve. Winter service chevrons shall be worn on the winter service coat and overcoat; summer service chevrons on khaki shirt and field jacket; and green summer chevrons on summer service, summer service L and summer dress coats.

CAP ORNAMENTS
96.
(a) The bronze cap ornament shall be worn on the winter service cap, and on the summer dress cap with summer parade uniform.
(b) The gilt cap ornament shall be worn on the summer dress cap with summer dress and summer undress uniforms.
(c) The left bronze collar ornament shall be worn on the garrison cap, on the left side, in the place provided therefor.
(d) The cap ornament shall be worn with the eagle up.

COLLAR ORNAMENTS
97.
(a) Bronze collar ornaments shall be worn on the winter service coat, centered on the collar between the crease roll and outer edge with center of hemisphere 1 inch above the horizontal edge of lapel notch, the vertical axis of ornament perpendicular, with eagle facing inside (see Plate 1, illustration No 2).
(b) Collar ornaments shall be worn on the summer dress coat, summer service coat, and summer service LS coat, centered on the collar at a point 3-1/4 inches from point of the collar measuring along the outside edge and 1-3/4 inches from the outside edge measuring toward notch, the vertical axis of ornament perpendicular, with eagle facing inside (see Plate 1, illustration No 4).
(c) Gilt collar ornaments shall be worn on the summer dress coat and on the summer service LS coat.
(d) Bronze collar ornaments shall be worn on the summer service coat and on the summer service LS coat, when prescribed as summer parade uniform.

MISCELLANEOUS (ENLISTED WOMEN)
98. The official mourning band, for pallbearers at military funerals only, shall be worn on the left sleeve (fastened at the back) midway between the armhole seam and the elbow, or directly below the chevron.

99. The sick list band shall be worn on the right sleeve midway between the shoulder seam and the elbow, or directly below the chevron.
100. Brassards shall be worn on the left sleeve (fastened at back), midway between the armhole seam and the elbow, or directly below the chevron.

CHAPTER VI
DECORATIONS, MEDALS, RIBBONS AND BADGES

110. Chapter VI, Uniform Regulations, United States Marine Corps, 1937, shall govern the wearing of decorations, medals, ribbons and badges by Women's Reserve officers and enlisted persons. In determining the proper location for attaching decorations, medals, ribbons and badges on coats with slanted upper pockets, a horizontal line tangent to the highest point of the slanted pocket shall be considered as the top of the pocket.

CHAPTER VII
TABLES OF UNIFORMS – COMMISSIONED OFFICERS

UNIFORM	CAP	COAT	SKIRT	BUTTONS	SHIRT	GLOVES
Winter dress (off duty)	Winter service (1)	Winter service (1)	Winter service (1)	Bronze	White (2)	Brown (3)
Winter service (duty, parade and optional off duty)	Winter service (1)	Winter service (1)	Winter service (1)	Bronze	Khaki (6)	Brown (3)
Summer dress (off duty)	Summer dress	Summer dress (11), (14)	Summer dress (11)	Gilt	--	White
Summer dress "A" (13) (off duty)	Summer dress	Summer dress "A" (11)	Summer dress A" (11)	Gilt	Summer dress A blouse	White
Summer undress (off duty)	Summer dress	Summer service LS (12), (14)	Summer service (12)	Green	--	White
Summer service (duty and optional off duty)	Summer dress or summer garrison	Summer service (12), (14)	Summer service (12) --	Green	--	White (13)
Summer parade	Summer dress (15)	Summer summer service or LS (12), (14), (16)	Summer service (12)	Green	--	White (16)

(1) Forestry green serge, covert, or other suitable cloth of adopted standard
(2) Green dress scarf
(3) Leather or fabric
(4) Lightweight raincoat optional
(5) When appropriate (prescribed muffler shall be worn with, but not without, overcoat, trench coat and lightweight raincoat)
(6) Khaki service scarf
(7) Omitted for parade
(8) Oxfords in ranks; pumps may be worn when engaged in office work and when off duty

HANDBAG	SHOES	HOSE	ORNAMENTS	OUTER COAT (5)	MUFFLER (5)
Brown	Brown pumps	Beige	Service	Overcoat or trench coat (4)	Red wool
Brown (7)	Brown (8)	Beige (9)	Service	Overcoat or trench coat (4) (10)	White rayon
With green cover & strap	White pumps	Beige	Dress	Trench coat (4)	White rayon
With green cover & strap	White pumps	Beige	Dress	Trench coat (4)	White rayon
With green cover & strap	White or brown pumps	Beige	Service or dress (17)	Trench coat (4)	White rayon
With green cover & strap	Brown (8)	Beige (9)	Service	Trench coat (4)	White rayon
(7)	Brown Oxfords	Beige (9)	Service	Trench coat	White rayon

(9) Lisle in ranks
(10) Trench coat or overcoat in ranks, at the discretion of the commanding officer
(11) White twill, tropical worsted, Palm Beach cloth or similar material
(12) Green and white stripe
(13) Wearing optional
(14) Green shoulder straps
(15) With bronze buttons
(16) At the discretion of the commanding officer
(17) Service ornaments with brown pumps, dress ornaments with white pumps

TABLES OF UNIFORMS – ENLISTED PERSONNEL

UNIFORM	CAP	COAT	SKIRT	BUTTONS	SHIRT	GLOVES
Winter dress (off duty)	Winter service (1)	Winter service (1)	Winter service (1)	Bronze	Khaki (2)	Brown (3)
Winter service (duty, parade and optional off duty)	Winter service (1)	Winter service (1)	Winter service (1)	Bronze	Khaki (2)	Brown (3)
Summer dress (off duty)	Summer dress	Summer dress (9)	Summer dress (9)	Gilt	--	White
Summer undress (off duty)	Summer dress	Summer service LS (10)	Summer service (10)	Green	--	White
Summer service (duty and optional off duty)	Summer garrison	Summer service (10)	Summer service (10)	Green	--	White (11)
Summer parade	Summer dress (13)	Summer service or summer service LS (10) (14)	Summer service (10)	Green	--	White (14)

(1) Forestry green serge or covert cloth
(2) Khaki service scarf
(3) Leather or fabric
(4) When appropriate (prescribed muffler shall be worn with, but not without, overcoat, trench coat, and lightweight raincoat)
(5) Omitted for parade
(6) Oxfords in ranks; pumps may be worn when engaged in office work and when off duty
(7) Lisle in ranks
(8) Trench coat or overcoat in ranks, at the discretion of the commanding officer
(9) White twill
(10) Green and white stripe
(11) Wearing optional
(12) Lightweight raincoat optional
(13) With bronze buttons
(14) At the discretion of the commanding officer

HANDBAG	SHOES	HOSE	ORNAMENTS	OUTER COAT(4)	MUFFLER (4)
Brown	Brown pumps	Beige	Bronze	Overcoat or trench coat (12)	Red wool
Brown (5)	Brown (6)	Beige (7)	Bronze	Overcoat or trench coat (8) (12)	Red wool
With green cover and strap	White pumps	Beige	Gilt	Trench coat (12)	White rayon
With green cover and strap	White or brown pumps	Beige	Gilt	Trench coat (12)	White rayon
With green cover and strap	Brown (6)	Beige (7)	Bronze	Trench coat (12)	White rayon
(5)	Brown Oxfords	Beige (7)	Bronze	Trench coat	White rayon

INDEX

	Paragraph number
Badges	110
Band, official mourning	
Commissioned officers	85
Enlisted persons	98
Specification	30
Band, sick list, enlisted persons	99
Bathing suits	47 (a)
Boots	34
Brassards, enlisted persons	100
Buttons	
Required	31(a)–(g)
Caps	32 (a), (b)
Chevrons	95
Civilian clothing	16
Commanding officer, responsibility of	8
Cover, rain, cap	32 (c)
Culottes	47 (b)
Decorations	110
Flowers	18
Galoshes	34
Gloves	
Brown	35 (a), (c)
Indoors, removal of	35 (e)
White	35 (b), (d)
Grooming	
Buttons	31 (h)
Colored nail polish	36 (c)
Hair	36 (b), (d)
Hose	39 (e)
Lipstick	36 (a)
Mascara	36 (b)
Rouge	36 (b)
Slips	36 (e), (f)
Handbag	37
Cover, green	37 (a)
strap	37 (a), (b)
Handkerchiefs	38
Hose	39
Insignia of rank	75-82, Plate 2

Captain	81
Colonel	79
First lieutenant	82
Lieutenant colonel	80
Major	80
Second lieutenant	82
Jacket, field	40, 47 (b), (c)
Jewelry	14
Medals	110
Mufflers	
Red	41 (a)
White	41 (b)
Ornaments	
Cap:	
Commissioned officers	42 (a), (b), 83
Enlisted persons	42 (c), (d), 96
Cap, garrison:	
Commissioned officers	77 (b) 83 (c)
Enlisted persons	96 (c)
Collar:	
Commissioned officers	42 (a), (b), 84
Illustration	Plate 1
Enlisted persons	42 (c), (d), 97
Illustration	Plate 1
Required	42
Overcoat	43, 48 (a)
Raincoat, lightweight	48 (c)
Optional possession of	2
Ribbons, service	110
Rubbers	34
Scarfs	
Dress	44 (b)
Service	44 (a)
Shirts	
Khaki	Chap VII
Utility	47 (b)
White	Chap VII
Shoes	
Oxfords	45 (a)
Pumps:	
Brown	45 (b)
White	45 (c)
Slacks	
Covert	47 (b)
Utility	47 (b)
Sports clothing	47

Strap, shoulder	
Green	76
Insignia of rank on	75, Plate 2
Substitutes for prescribed articles	7
Suit, exercise	47 (b)
Trench coat	48 (a), (b)
Umbrellas	15
Uniform	
Ceremonies, appropriate for	60
Changes in regulations, when effective	9
Combination of	3
Dress A summer	Chap VII
Optional possession of	2
Ornaments	84 (e), Plate 2
Dress, summer	Chap VII
Dress, winter	Chap VII
Fitting of	13
Inspection of	8, 12
Liberty	61
Maintenance of:	
Commissioned officers	11
Enlisted persons	12,13
Occasions on which each uniform is to be worn	Chap III
Official	60
Parade	64, Chap VII
Social	60, 61
Of the day	4, 5, 6
Off duty	Chap VII
Commissioned officers	61
Enlisted persons	61
Officers suspended, not to be worn by	10
On duty	60, 65, 66, Chap VII
Procurement duty	62, 63
Required articles of	2
Service	Chaps III, VII
Summer	62, 63, 66
Winter	60, 62, 63, 64, 65
Skirts	
Length of	46 (a)
Seams, pressing of	46 (b)
Tables of	Chap VII
Tailor made	17
Undress, summer	62, 63
Uniformity required, officers and enlisted persons	3
Weddings	16
Work clothes	49
Inspection of	8

LIST OF ILLUSTRATIONS

                                                              Plate

Ornaments, collar   1
Officers
Enlisted women

Ornaments, collar and insignia of rank
Officer's summer dress A uniform   2

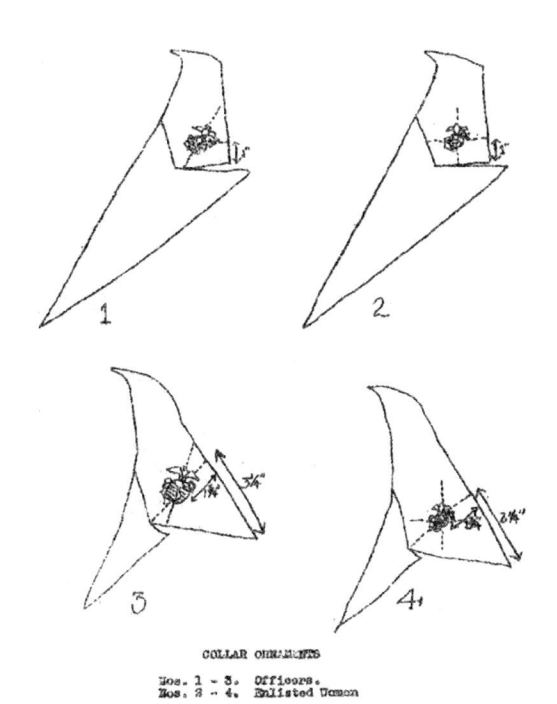

Plate 1 – collar ornaments

Plate 2 (revised)
Officers Summer Dress A: Ornament and insignia of rank on shoulder strap.